The Holy Spirit: Friend and Counselor

by
Milton S. Agnew

Beacon Hill Press of Kansas City
Kansas City, Missouri

Permission to quote from the following copyrighted versions of the Bible is acknowledged with appreciation:

The *Amplified New Testament* (Amp.), © 1958 by the Lockman Foundation.

The *Good News Bible—Today's English Version* (TEV), Old Testament © American Bible Society, 1976; New Testament © American Bible Society, 1966, 1971, 1976.

The Living Bible (TLB), © 1971 by Tyndale House Publishers, Wheaton, Ill.

New American Standard Bible (NASB), © The Lockman Foundation, 1960, 1962, 1968, 1971, 1972, 1973, 1975.

New English Bible (NEB), © The Delegates of the Oxford University Press and The Syndics of the Cambridge University Press, 1961, 1970.

The Holy Bible, New International Version (NIV), copyright © 1978 by the New York International Bible Society.

New Testament in Modern English (Phillips), Revised Edition © J. B. Phillips 1958, 1960, 1972. By permission of the Macmillan Publishing Co., Inc.

New Testament in the Language of the People (Williams), copyright 1937 by Bruce Humphries, Inc. Assigned 1949 to Moody Bible Institute, Chicago.

Revised Standard Version of the Bible (RSV), copyrighted 1946, 1952, © 1971, 1973.

Contents

Preface

We here present an effort to make personal the presence and personality of the Holy Spirit. In many respects He is the neglected member of the Trinity, yet indispensable in His responsibilities, and inimitable in His care and concern.

This is not basically a record of personal experiences of God's saints in relation to the Spirit, although some of that is a viable part of the thesis. It represents, rather, a reasoned effort to exhibit a Scripture-based, orderly presentation of the Holy Spirit, both in the days of the Old Covenant, and now, under the auspices of the New Covenant which was sealed by the shed blood of Jesus and established at His glorification. It seeks to show that the Holy Spirit is profoundly active today in the world, in the Church, and in the hearts of His people.

We dedicate this treatise to the committed servants of God scattered across four continents with whom we have had the privilege of working these recent years in conferences and in institutes directed particularly to the Person and work of the Holy Spirit in the lives of the children of God.

—MILTON S. AGNEW

1/

OUR MYSTIC GOD

Years ago when Mark Twain was in Berlin he received an invitation asking him to call upon the Kaiser. "Why, Dad," exclaimed his little daughter after rereading the note in speechless awe, "if it keeps on this way there won't be anybody left for you to get acquainted with but God." An amusing remark it was, but possibly one bearing some sad implications for many people for whom God is not in the circle of intimate acquaintance.

However, to those of us in a Judeo-Christian environment the general concept of God is quite familiar. God is the Head of the universe, the Creator of the heavens and the earth. In an entirely unexplainable way He is eternal. He is without a beginning—"In the beginning God" (Gen. 1:1), and without an end or termination—"Even from everlasting to everlasting, thou art God" (Ps. 90:2).

To those of us subscribing to the Christian tradition, God is indeed the Head of our spiritual household. He is the Creator. He is also the Father who so loved that He sent His Son to die for us. The Father-God figure is entirely familiar to us, and needs no further introduction. God the Son is our most intimate touch with the Godhead. We have known Him as a winsome Child. We grew up with Him through the trying years of youth, to the responsible days of manhood. "He was in all points tempted" even as we are. He understands us, and we Him. We love Him.

But the Spirit? Who is He? How do we understand Him? To what can we relate Him in our human experience? He is different. To us He is the mystic member of the Godhead. We are inclined to think of Him as being unrealistic, impersonal, merely a spirit or essence. We use the terms, "The spirit of God," "the spirit of Christ," "the spirit of the Lord," "my spirit," "the spirit of truth." But who is He?

1. He Is a Person

Part of the difficulty in recognizing the Holy Spirit as a Person is the lofty, *impersonal* concept generally projected for the word *spirit*. Funk and Wagnalls *Standard College Dictionary* (1977) declares: "**Spirit.** The vital essence or animating force in living organisms, especially man." A "vital essence" and an "animating force" do not exactly put Him into the same category with "The Father God," with "God the Son." And the further definitions do not help: "The part of a human being that is incorporeal and self-conscious. The substance or universal aspect of reality. In the Bible, the creative, animating power or divine influence of God." Thus He is recognized by all too many as only "a creative animating power, a divine influence"—but not as a Person. The dictionary says He is but a "power," a "divine influence." That's all!

Unfortunately, the old English of the King James Version, has, in addition, presented Him as "the Holy Ghost." "Ghost," the dictionary declares is: "1. A disembodied spirit; a wraith, specter, or phantom; 2. The animating spirit or soul; 3. A haunting recollection of something; 4. A mere shadow, trace, or suggestion of something." What concepts are bound to arise in a 20th-century mind! To say the least, this has confused many. In a deeper sense it has contributed to an aura of unreality, of question, of myth in relation to the Third Person of the Trinity.

But to the Holy Spirit are ascribed by the Scriptures all the attributes of personality. In the Old Testament He was the partner of God in creation: "The spirit of God moved upon the face of the waters" (Gen. 1:2); and "The spirit of God hath made me" (Job 33:4). It is recorded that "the spirit of the Lord came upon" individuals like Gideon (Judg. 6:34) and David (1 Sam. 16:13). He was identified in Isa. 63:10-11 as "his holy spirit" (lower case in the King James but capitalized in NIV and others). Gradually God the Holy Spirit was being identified as a Person. In the New Testament He is accorded many additional attributes of personality: that of knowing (Rom. 8:27), of feeling (Eph. 4:30), of willing (1 Cor. 12:11), and all manner of personal actions such as hearing, speaking, guiding, bestowing gifts.

The Holy Spirit *is* a Divine Person—Indeed one of the three Persons in the Godhead.

2. He Is a Member of the Trinity

How can there be three Persons in the Godhead? Deuteronomy 6:4 plainly declares "The Lord our God is one Lord." However, this can be true in the same sense that a man and wife, on marriage, become one, yet remain two persons. "Therefore shall a man leave his father and his mother, and shall cleave unto his wife" is declared in the Scriptures in Gen. 2:24, and endorsed by Jesus in Matt. 19:4-5: "They shall be one flesh." Furthermore, He is a very active Member of the Trinity.

That there is a plurality of the Godhead was intimated in the days of old with such plural identification as "God said, Let *us* make man in *our* image, after *our* likeness" (Gen. 1:26, italics added), and in Isaiah's record "I heard the voice of the Lord, saying, Whom shall I send, and who will go for us?" (6:8). It would seem that it is the Second Person of the Godhead speaking as He recognized the Trinity, in the statement, "The Lord God has sent Me, and His Spirit" (Isa. 48:16, NASB). And, as recorded in Luke 4:18-21, Jesus is accepting as authentic regarding himself and the Holy Spirit the statement as recorded in Luke 4:18-21, made by Isaiah in 61:1-2, "The spirit of the Lord God is upon me; because the Lord hath anointed me to preach good tidings unto the meek; he hath sent me to bind up the brokenhearted, to proclaim liberty to the captives, and the opening of the prison to them that are bound; to proclaim the acceptable year of the Lord, and the day of vengeance of our God; to comfort all that mourn." To this Jesus added, "This day is this scripture fulfilled in your ears."

However, nowhere do we find the prophets under the Old Covenant clearly presenting the Trinity.

It was New Testament times before the Holy Spirit was clearly identified as a Member of the Trinity. Two mystical appearances are recorded. To Mary the angel said, "The Holy Ghost shall come upon thee, and the power of the Highest shall overshadow thee" (Luke 1:35). Then at the baptism of Jesus, the voice of God the Father came from heaven: "This is my beloved Son, in whom I am well pleased," and God the Holy Spirit descended "like a dove, and lighted upon him" (Matt. 3:16-17). Yet

8

still the Holy Spirit was clothed in mystery—"descending like a dove."

Nevertheless, as the New Testament unfolded, it revealed the reality of the Trinity which had been but a shadow in the Old. Jesus clearly presents this in His great commission, "Baptizing them in the name of the Father, and of the Son, and of the Holy Ghost" (Matt. 28:19). Luke recognizes the Trinity in his description of the death of Stephen who "being full of the Holy Ghost," Luke declares, "looked up stedfastly into heaven, and saw the glory of God, and Jesus standing on the right hand of God, and said, Behold I see the heavens opened, and the Son of man standing on the right hand of God" (Acts 7:55-56). Also, Paul concludes his second letter to the Corinthians with the trinitarian benediction: "The grace of the Lord Jesus Christ, and the love of God, and the communion of the Holy Ghost, be with you all" (2 Cor. 13:14).

3. There Are Symbols with Respect to Him

That the Holy Spirit is associated with symbols further deepens the mystique of His personality. There are none representing the Father. There are none representing the Son save one—the Lamb of God. But the Spirit has numerous symbols. This may accent the mystery aspect, but the symbols are meaningful identifications. We have already noted the association with a dove, but let us note some others.

a. He is symbolized by breath and by wind. In both the Hebrew and the Greek languages three distinct but interrelated meanings (breath, wind, and spirit) are covered by one word—*ruach* in the Hebrew, and *pneuma* in the Greek. These are translated "breath" in Gen. 2:7 and Acts 17:25; "wind" in Gen. 8:1 and John 3:8; "spirit" in Gen. 1:2; 6:3; and John 3:8.

Thus He is the "breath" of God. God "breathes" the

9

Holy Spirit. When Job declared (33:4): "The spirit of the Lord hath made me, and the breath of the Almighty hath given me life" he was commenting directly on the record in Gen. 2:7, "The Lord God formed man of the dust of the ground, and breathed into his nostrils the breath of life; and man became a living soul." Through the instrumentality of the Holy Spirit as the breath of God, man was created for immortality!

In the New Testament, Jesus used this symbolism to present the new birth of regeneration. "Marvel not that I said unto thee, Ye must be born again. The wind bloweth where it listeth, and thou hearest the sound thereof, but canst not tell whence it cometh, and whither it goeth: so is every one that is born of the Spirit" (John 3:7-8). Contemplate our "mystic God." He who gave to man the breath of immortality brings now the breath of eternal life.

Ezekiel had counted the Spirit as the breath of God, related to God's people, when he described his "vision of dry bones" (chap. 37). "Behold I will cause breath to enter into you, and ye shall live" (v. 5). Then follows the prophecy: "(I) shall put my spirit in you, and ye shall live" (v. 14). The "bones" which represented "the whole house of Israel," would come alive with this infusion of the Spirit of God.

It is from this symbolism that we get such meaningful songs as:

> Breathe on me, Breath of God;
>   Fill me with life anew,
> That I may love what Thou dost love,
>   And do what Thou wouldst do.
> —EDWIN HATCH

b. The symbolism of the Spirit as *water* is of deep theological significance. Jesus made the mystical statement "If any man thirst, let him come unto me, and drink.

10

He that believeth on me . . . out of his belly shall flow rivers of living water." To which John made supplemental comment in recording this many years later, "This spake he of the Spirit, which they that believe on him should receive" (John 7:37-39).

c. The symbolism of the Spirit as *oil* is twofold. As that which dedicates by an anointing, oil was used to consecrate the priest: "Then thou shalt take the anointing oil, and pour it on his head, and anoint him" (Exod. 29:7). Oil was also used to anoint the king (1 Sam. 12:3-5). Jesus, as Prophet, Priest and King, boldly declared at the commencement of His ministry: "The Spirit of the Lord is upon me, because he hath anointed me to preach the gospel" (Luke 4:18); while Peter later declared of Him, "God anointed Jesus of Nazareth with the Holy Ghost and with power: who went about doing good, and healing all that were oppressed of the devil; for God was with him" (Acts 10:38). Paul had reference to the same action by the Holy Spirit upon believers when he declared, "He which stablisheth us with you in Christ, and hath anointed us, is God, who hath also sealed us, and given the earnest of the Spirit in our hearts" (2 Cor. 1:21-22). John expressed it, "Ye have an unction [*chrisma*] from the Holy One. . . . But the anointing [*chrisma*] which ye have received of him abideth in you" (1 John 2:20, 27). It is indeed a blessed experience to be—with Christ—an "anointed" servant of our God.

But the Holy Spirit is represented by oil under another aspect when Jesus gave the parable of the wise and foolish virgins. Matthew 25:1-8 (NASB) says in part, "When the foolish took their lamps, they took no oil with them, but the prudent took oil in flasks along with their lamps." Then, the midnight cry of the unwise, "Our lamps are going out," or are being quenched, reminds us of the warning given by Paul, "Quench not the Spirit" (1 Thess.

11

5:19). For this supply of oil, representing that inward grace which distinguishes the wise, must denote, more particularly, that supply of the Spirit of Jesus which, as it is the source of the new spiritual life at the first, is the secret of its enduring character. The supply of oil is not automatically renewed; it requires care from the possessor. It is in that sense that Paul admonishes, "Ever be filled with the Spirit" (Eph. 5:18, Williams). The present imperative of "be filled" presents an ongoing process which must characterize the prudent believer.

d. Another very significant symbolism for the Holy Spirit is *fire*. John made the meaningful proclamation, "I indeed baptize you with water unto repentance: but he that cometh after me is mightier than I, whose shoes I am not worthy to bear: he shall baptize you with the Holy Ghost, and with fire" (Matt. 3:11-12). It might be noted that the preposition "with" is not repeated in the Greek, therefore the second "with" is in italics in the KJV, and is omitted in the NASB. Thus the force of the Greek indicates that "fire" is synonymous with "the Holy Ghost"—"the Holy Ghost and [even] fire."

What, then, is the significance of equating the Spirit with fire? It is not the fire of the final judgment referred to in v. 12 when He will "burn up the chaff with unquenchable fire," nor as in 2 Thess. 1:8, "In flaming fire taking vengeance on them that know not God, and that obey not the gospel of our Lord Jesus Christ."

Rather He is the fire that cleanses. Hebrews 12:29 reads, "Our God is a consuming fire." He is the fire that tries and proves. First Peter 1:7 speaks of "the trial of your faith, being much more precious than of gold that perisheth, though it be tried with fire."

I recall an experience which made a profound impression on my life many years ago. I was selling The Salvation Army *War Cry*, and had entered a small shop. Upon my re-

12

quest of the proprietor that he might buy a copy he asked me to wait a moment as he completed a task he was involved in. I noted the Bunsen burner and the small beaker containing some liquid with which he was working.

"May I ask what you are doing?" I inquired.

"Purifying gold," was the reply. He paused a moment, then added, "See the dark impurities which come to the surface? I now remove them with this small ladle."

I watched as he patiently waited for more dark spots to appear. As he removed one more I inquired, "When do you know the gold is pure?"

There was a further short pause. "When I can see my face reflected in the gold, then it is pure."

I learned a lasting lesson. "When the Holy Spirit can see His face reflected in my life, then it is pure." (P.S. He did buy the *War Cry*.)

The Holy Spirit is the fire that empowers. "John truly baptized with water: but ye shall be baptized with the Holy Ghost not many days hence . . . But ye shall receive power, after that the Holy Ghost is come upon you" (Acts 1:5-8).

Writes Thomas Lynch:

> *Mighty Spirit, dwell with me;*
> *I myself would mighty be,*
> *Mighty so as to prevail*
> *Where unaided man must fail;*
> *Ever by a mighty hope*
> *Pressing on and bearing up.*

And this amazing power is available to the believer. Years ago a vessel sank in the Hudson River. It was imperative that it be lifted and towed away, for it was obstructing the channel into New York harbor. Several engineers attempted to raise it but failed. One day a man said, "I am no engineer, but I believe I can move the sunken ship." He assembled a number of barges on either

13

side of the vessel and, at low tide, strung powerful chains under the hull and fastened them securely to the barges. When the tide began to rise, the sunken vessel was automatically lifted and then towed away. This man succeeded because he harnessed up the mighty power of the ocean. "Ye shall receive power after that the Holy Ghost is come upon you."

He is also the fire that illuminates and enlightens— who will "guide you into all truth" (John 16:13).

> O send Thy Spirit, Lord,
>   Now unto me,
> That He may touch my eyes
>   And make me see;
> Show me the truth concealed
>   Within Thy Word,
> And in Thy Book revealed
>   I see the Lord.
>   —ALEXANDER GROVES

Again, He is the fire that ignites, kindles, inflames. "Who maketh his ministers a flaming fire" (Heb. 1:7). How impatient God must be with the tepid Christian! "Because thou art lukewarm, and neither cold nor hot, I will spue thee out of my mouth" (Rev. 3:16), declares the Lord our God.

Charles Wesley has given us an urgent prayer:

> My God! I know, I feel Thee mine,
>   And will not quit the claim
> Till all I have is lost in Thine,
>   And all renewed I am.
>
> O that in me the sacred fire
>   Might now begin to glow,
> Burn up the dross of base desire,
>   And make the mountains flow!

> *O that it now from Heaven might fall,*
> *And all my sins consume!*
> *Come, Holy Ghost, for Thee I call,*
> *Spirit of burning, come!*

And who has not thrilled as he joins the congregation in the climactic last verse!

> *Refining fire, go through my heart,*
> *Illuminate my soul;*
> *Scatter Thy life through every part,*
> *And sanctify the whole.*

It is, of course, from this fire of the Holy Spirit and the blood of Christ that the Salvation Army takes its terse motto, inscribed on its flag: "BLOOD and FIRE."

As meaningful as these symbols of the Holy Spirit may be, they may tend to depersonalize Him. Unfortunately the King James Version speaks of "the Spirit itself" (Rom. 8:26), and "it abode upon him" (John 1:32). This is due to a slavish following of the Greek where *pneuma,* spirit, is neuter in gender and the Greek pronoun follows suit. Fortunately, all the modern translations have corrected this KJV error. Jesus very carefully always used the masculine personal pronoun when speaking of the Spirit, as in John 16:7, 8, 13, 14; 14:17, 26; 15:26. To Jesus, the Spirit was "He" and "Who," never "it" or "that."

4. The Holy Spirit Offers and Desires Fellowship

The very warmth of this marks the Holy Spirit as a Friend. Second Corinthians 13:14 states: "The grace of the Lord Jesus Christ, and the love of God, and the fellowship of the Holy Spirit, be with you all" (NASB), while Phil. 2:1 declares: "If therefore there is any encouragement in Christ, if there is any consolation of love, if there is any fellowship of the Spirit, if any affection and compassion, make my joy complete by being of the same mind"

15

(NASB). The Greek word here is *koinonia*, which is derived from *koinonos*, meaning a partner, associate, companion, as in 2 Cor. 8:23 where Titus is listed as Paul's *partner* and fellow-helper, and in Philem. 17 where Paul would be counted as a *partner* to Philemon; meaning also partaker or sharer as in 2 Pet. 1:4, "Whereby are given unto us exceeding great and precious promises: that by these ye might be partakers of the divine nature."

Thus He, the Holy Spirit, offers and seeks partnership, companionship, and desires that we be partakers or sharers with Him.

Then the word also means *fellowship*, manifested in acts wrought by the Holy Spirit through the lives of believers. These acts or ministries are the practical effects of fellowship with God. "I pray that the fellowship of your faith may become effective through the knowledge of every good thing which is in you for Christ's sake" (Philem. 6, NASB).

Albert Orsborn caught something of the significance of this fellowship in his song.

> Spirit of eternal love,
> Guide me, or I blindly rove;
> Set my heart on things above,
>   Draw me after Thee.
> Earthly things are paltry show,
> Phantom charms, they come and go;
> Give me constantly to know
>   Fellowship with Thee.
>
> Come, O Spirit, take control
> Where the fires of passion roll;
> Let the yearnings of my soul
>   Center all in Thee.
> Call into Thy fold of peace
> Thoughts that seek forbidden ways;

Calm and order all my days,
  Hide my life in Thee.

Thus supported, even I,
Knowing Thee for ever nigh,
Shall attain that deepest joy,
  Living unto Thee.
No distracting thoughts within,
No surviving hidden sin,
Thus shall Heaven indeed begin
  Here and now in me.

Fellowship with Thee,
Fellowship with Thee,
  Give me constantly to know
Fellowship with Thee.

5. There Are Evidences of His Divinity

The divinity of this Third Person of the Trinity is evidenced in several ways. For example, disobedience to Him is disobedience to God. Peter asked Ananias, "Why hath Satan filled thine heart to lie to the Holy Ghost. . . ? thou hast not lied unto men, but unto God" (Acts 5:3-4).

His omnipresence must also be noted. The Psalmist wrote, "Whither shall I go from thy Spirit? or whither shall I flee from thy presence? . . . If I take the wings of the morning, and dwell in the uttermost parts of the sea; even there shall thy hand lead me, and thy right hand shall hold me. If I say, Surely the darkness shall cover me; even the night shall be light about me. Yea, the darkness hideth not from thee; but the night shineth as the day: the darkness and the light are both alike to thee" (Ps. 139:7-12).

His omniscience is reflected in His knowledge. "The thoughts of God no one knows, except the Spirit of God" (1 Cor. 2:11, NASB).

His omnipotence is reflected in the miracle of the Resurrection. "If the Spirit of him that raised up Jesus from the dead dwell in you, he that raised up Christ from the dead shall also quicken your mortal bodies by his Spirit" (Rom. 8:11). It is also seen in the marvel of the new birth. "That which is born of the flesh is flesh; and that which is born of the Spirit is spirit" (John 3:6). It is further apparent in man's deliverance: "The law of the Spirit of life in Christ Jesus hath made me free from the law of sin and death" (Rom. 8:2).

6. He Can Be Affected by Our Attitude Toward Him

a. He can be made sad. "Grieve not the Holy Spirit of God" (Eph. 4:30), commands Paul. Now, only a dear friend can be grieved. Not a stranger: he might be annoyed. Not a chance acquaintance: he might be perplexed. Not a business partner: he might be offended. Only a loved one can be grieved. This very expression brings the Holy Spirit close to us in an intimate relationship. Without sacrificing the majesty of His divinity, it etches with new clarity the reality of His personality. He isn't just the Third Person of the Godhead, a mysterious entity. He is our loving Partner. And how may He be grieved? The context of verses 31 and 32 suggests ways: by expressing "bitterness ... wrath ... anger ... clamour ... slander ... all malice," attitudes and actions which mar any household. He is tender of spirit, conscious of strife, grieved at our selfish ways.

> *Tender Spirit, dwell with me;*
> *I myself would tender be;*
> *Tender in my love for men,*
> *Wooing them to God again;*
> *With compassion pure and sweet*
> *Lead the lost to Jesus' feet.*

b. He can be vexed. This is stronger than grieved.

18

"They rebelled, and vexed his Holy Spirit: therefore he was turned to be their enemy, and he fought against them" (Isa. 63:10). These are strong words. But they come out of strong provocation. "In all their affliction he was afflicted," says the previous verse, "and the angel of his presence saved them: in his love and in his pity he redeemed them; and he bare them and carried them all the days of old. *But they rebelled and vexed his holy Spirit*" (italics added). God can be vexed. To vex means "to disturb, nervously upset, annoy, or anger as by petty provocation." These things the children of Israel had done. And the Holy Spirit was vexed. But more, much more, "He was turned to be their enemy, and he fought against them," continues the Scripture. This is akin to an exhibition of the "wrath of God." God the Holy Spirit is not to be treated as a nonentity. How fearful to have Him as our "enemy," to have Him "fight against" us!

c. He may be omnipotent, but He is not autocratic. He can be successfully resisted. "Ye stiffnecked and uncircumcised in heart and ears," cried out Stephen in his accusations, "ye do always resist the Holy Ghost: as your fathers did, so do ye" (Acts 7:51). Although divinely omnipotent, in respecting man's freedom of choice and ultimate responsibility, the Spirit will not impose His omnipotence on those who resolutely resist Him. And, since, as we shall see, the Holy Spirit has a vital ministry in man's salvation in all its facets, this resistance can be serious, even eternally lethal.

d. He may be omniscient, but can be lied to, though not deceived. Peter's question to Ananias is an example: "Why hath Satan filled thine heart to lie to the Holy Ghost?" (Acts 5:3). Men may falsify the truth to the Spirit, but not successfully.

e. Further, as we have previously noted, the Holy Spirit can be quenched. As NIV expresses it, "Do not put out the Spirit's fire" (1 Thess. 5:19). This, apparently, is done by failure to renew a supply of the Holy Spirit (Matt. 25:1-13), by failure to "keep filled" with the Spirit (Eph. 5:18). It can be done by failure to "kindle afresh" (NASB), to "fan into a flame" (NIV), to "stir up" (KJV) the gift of God (2 Tim. 1:6-7).

> *Sweet Spirit of Christ,*
> *Make my poor heart Thy dwelling,*
> *Thy beauty adorning,*
> *Other souls draw nigh to Thee.*

2/

JESUS AND THE
HOLY SPIRIT

Who, according to Jesus, is this mystic Third Person of the Trinity? What are His characteristics? Where do we find Him? How is He related to us?

Jesus recognized the Holy Spirit in several duties and patterns. It was the Spirit who had anointed Him for service (Luke 4:14-21), and this in fulfillment of God's long-range plan announced some 600 years before by Isaiah (61:1-2). It was the Holy Spirit who would bring spiritual birth to those dead in sins (John 3:5-6). Pursuing the symbolism of water as the Holy Spirit, it was the Spirit who would be living water, springing up into everlasting life (John 4:10-14), and who would fill to overflowing the believer who would receive Him in His fullness (John 7:37-39). He would also be available to the believer upon request to His Heavenly Father (Luke 11:13).

1. As the Paraclete

Of particular interest is Jesus' reference to the Holy Spirit as "The Paraclete," as recorded in John 14, 15, and 16, and as variously translated "the Comforter" (KJV), the "Helper" (NASB), the "Counselor" (NIV), the "Advocate" (NEB), "someone else to stand by you" (Phillips), the "Intercessor," "Strengthener," "Standby" (Amplified). According to etymology, the *parakletos* is "one called to one's side" (*para* = alongside; *kletos* = called). Thus He is one who can be called alongside for these various reasons—to comfort, to help, to counsel, to enlighten, to cause to remember, to stand by, to intercede, to strengthen, to encourage, to exhort, to console. As can be seen, no one translation is sufficient for the word. He is the Paraclete.

In this title Jesus has identified the Holy Spirit as having a personality and a purpose, with a profile of interesting usefulness. He has removed Him from impersonal symbolism, from mystic unreality, and has clothed Him with activity and purpose, friendliness and warmth. It is in the light of this identification that He may well be termed a Friend.

Samuel Longfellow catches something of this in his song:

> Holy Spirit, truth divine,
> Dawn upon this soul of mine;
> Word of God and inward light,
> Wake my spirit, clear my sight.
>
> Holy Spirit, love divine,
> Glow within this heart of mine;

Kindle every high desire,
Perish self in Thy pure fire.

We must look to the Scriptures themselves to learn of the Holy Spirit's duties, His position, and His possibilities as the Paraclete. There are essentially four "Paraclete Sayings"—John 14:15-17; 14:25-26; 15:26-27; 16:7-15. Since they constitute Jesus' major teachings about the Holy Spirit they are important.

    a. The first saying contains several pertinent truths.

> If ye love me, keep my commandments. And I will pray the Father and he shall give you another Comforter, that he may abide with you for ever; even the Spirit of truth; whom the world cannot receive, because it seeth him not, neither knoweth him: but ye know him; for he dwelleth with you, and shall be in you (John 14:15-17).

The Holy Spirit is "another" Comforter. This refers to the fact that Jesus, himself, is elsewhere identified, under the word *advocate,* as a paraclete in 1 John 2:1: "We have an advocate with the Father, Jesus Christ the righteous." And He is "another"—*allos,* which means of a similar character, not *heteros,* or dissimilar character (see Gal. 1:6). Thus the Christian has two Paracletes of the same nature, one called alongside by the Father to there present our cause, and the other called alongside by the believer to render the many services which are His.

Again, while Jesus would be departing this world, the Holy Spirit would remain—"that he may abide with you for ever." This promise has been misunderstood. Some have declared that no Spirit-filled child of God now need ever pray the prayer of David, "Take not thy holy spirit from me" (Ps. 51:11), for Jesus said, "He [will] abide with you for ever." But actually Jesus is not giving a promise of "eternal security" to a believer. This "you" is plural. He is contrasting the two facts—that He himself is departing, but that the Spirit is remaining. This is the age of the Holy Spirit for the Church. For while the Spirit—the Paraclete—is credited with both personality and deity, at the same time the Spirit is the Spirit of Jesus himself, for Jesus said, "I am the way, the truth, and the life." Thus He could also say, "I will not leave you as orphans; I will come to you" (John 14:18; NASB).

"Whom the world cannot receive." The inability of the world (the unsaved) "to receive" the Holy Spirit is an important pronouncement. On the other hand the inference is here given, and later the command clearly given, that believers should receive Him (John 20:22). The exact meaning of the word "receive" will be considered later. But His unavailability to the unsaved means that He is, in a peculiar sense, related uniquely and *only* to the child of God. In this regard Jesus additionally declared that while the Holy Spirit now dwelt "with" believers He would be "in" them.

b. The second paraclete statement speaks of teaching and of reminding.

> These things have I spoken unto you, being yet present with you. But the Comforter, which is the Holy Ghost, whom the Father will send in my name, he shall teach you all things, and bring all things to your remembrance, whatsoever I have said unto you (John 14:25-26).

For the disciples this had a direct bearing on the recording of the New Testament accounts of the Holy Spirit's ministry, a direct bearing on the inspiration of the New Testament. The full importance of this assurance would slowly dawn on them in the years to come as they were enabled to recall with accuracy the acts and words of Jesus. For all believers it gives promise of instruction and of understanding in the things of God and in the true meaning of the Scriptures.

c. The third saying deals with the important subject of the reinforcement of witness.

> When the Comforter is come, whom I will send unto you from the Father, even the Spirit of truth, which proceedeth from the Father, he shall testify of me: and ye also shall bear witness, because ye have been with me from the beginning (John 15:26-27).

Jesus was later to add to this the statement recorded in Acts 1:8: "But ye shall receive power, after that the Holy Ghost is come upon you: and ye shall be witnesses unto me both in Jerusalem, and in Samaria, and unto the uttermost part of the earth." A very important element of that power to witness effectively would be *the co-witness* of the Holy Spirit.

The need of at least two witnesses had long been established. "One witness shall not rise up against a man for any iniquity," said the law in Deut. 19:15, "or for any sin, in any sin that he sinneth: at the mouth of two witnesses, or at the mouth of three witnesses, shall the matter be established." Again, in Deut. 17:6, "At the mouth of two witnesses, or three witnesses, shall he that is worthy of death be put to death; but at the mouth of one witness he shall not be put to death." Jesus, in a New Testament ruling, declared: "Moreover if thy brother shall trespass against thee, go and tell him his fault between thee and him alone: if he shall hear thee, thou hast gained thy brother. But if he will not hear thee, then take with thee one or two more, that in the mouth of two or three witnesses every word may be established" (Matt. 18:15-16).

Jesus said of himself: "If I bear witness of myself, my witness is not true. There is another that beareth witness of me; and I know that the witness which he witnesseth of me is true. Ye sent unto John, and he bare witness unto the truth. . . . But I have greater witness than that of John. . . . The Father himself, which hath sent me, hath borne witness of me" (John 5:31-37; see also John 8:12-18). Paul added: "In the mouth of two or three witnesses shall every word be established" (2 Cor. 13:1).

Thus may be seen the importance of the corroborating witness of the Spirit to the witness of His children. "He shall testify of me: and ye also shall bear witness." The believer's witness will not stand alone, but will be supplemented and supported by His witness.

d. The fourth and longest of the paraclete sayings contains much important information. John 16:7-15 reads:

> Nevertheless I tell you the truth; it is expedient for you that I go away: for if I go not away, the Comforter will not come unto you; but if I depart, I will send him unto you. And when he is come, he will reprove the world of sin, and of righteousness, and of judgment: of sin, because they believe not on me; of righteousness, because I go to my Father, and ye see me no more; of judgment, because the prince of this world is judged.
>
> I have many things to say unto you, but ye cannot bear them now. Howbeit when he, the Spirit of truth is come, he will guide you into all truth: for he shall not speak of himself; but whatsoever he shall hear, that shall he speak: and he will shew you things to come. He will glorify me: for he shall receive of mine, and shall shew it unto you. All things that the Father hath are mine: therefore said I, that he shall take of mine, and shall shew it unto you.

It was more important for the Holy Spirit to come than for Jesus to stay—undoubtedly quite contrary to the urgent requests and protests of the disciples. Who could be more important to their welfare than Jesus? Indeed, what could they possibly do if He left them?

Jesus' answer was threefold—What the Holy Spirit, when He had come, would mean to the world; what He would mean to them as believers; and what He would mean to Jesus.

To the world He would bring conviction—conviction

regarding the shocking reality of sin, regarding the glorious possibility of righteousness, and regarding the terrifying truth of judgment.

Conviction is designated by the verb "reprove" (KJV), "convince" (RSV), "convict" (NASB, NIV), "confute" (NEB). These are from the verb *elenchō,* which is, according to G. Abbott-Smith[1] "a rebuke which brings conviction" (Matt. 18:15; Titus 1:9; John 8:46). This is in contrast to *epitimō,* which is "a rebuke which may be undeserved (Matt. 16:22), or is ineffectual" (Luke 23:40). The Paraclete will bring effectual conviction on the world regarding three important facts.

When He is come He will *convict the world of sin,* particularly of that chief sin, the sin of unbelief. For it is only by faith in the Lord Jesus Christ that man can be saved.

He will *convict the world of righteousness*—that righteousness of Christ which has been validated by His resurrection and ascension, and which is shown to be a practical reality in the lives of Spirit-filled men. See Rom. 12:1-2; Heb. 9:24-26; 12:5-10.

He will *convict the world that there is a day of accounting,* an eternal penalty for sin, as announced by Jesus in Matt. 25:32, by Peter in Acts 17:30, and by Paul in Rom. 14:10-12 and 2 Cor. 5:10. Satan himself has already been so judged.

When He has come to believers they will find in Him the Revealer of truth, the Unveiler of the mysteries of God's counsels. "He will not speak on His own iniative," says the NASB, "but whatever He hears, He will speak; and He will disclose to you what is to come." In an awesome sense Jesus promised insights into the very counsels of God.

When He has come to believers He will glorify Jesus through them. And this is the most important result of all—both for the Spirit himself, and for the Spirit-filled believer. Thus Jesus will be glorified.

Possibly the most exciting of all is that these activities of the Paraclete should all be accomplished through humble believers, *when they became recipients in full of the Holy Spirit, when they had called Him alongside.* It was to mark the bursting into view of a new age, the age of Spirit-filled believers being used by an almighty God. And that age is *now*.

3/

THE DIVINE
ADMINISTRATOR

The Members of the Trinity share interrelated activities, of which God the Holy Spirit is the Administrator.

1. He Was Active in Creation

In many ways the Holy Spirit had been evident as the Administrator of the Godhead from the beginning. It had been so at creation. Nature had been His handiwork. The writer of Genesis expressed it, "The Spirit of God was moving over the surface of the waters" (Gen. 1:2, NASB). The Psalmist echoes, "When you send your Spirit, they are created, and you renew the face of the earth" (Ps. 104:30, NIV). While, as previously noted, the record of Gen. 2:7,

"The Lord God formed man of the dust of the ground, and breathed into his nostrils the breath of life; and man became a living soul," is echoed in the words of Elihu, "The spirit of God hath made me, and the breath of the Almighty hath given me life. . . . I also am formed out of the clay" (Job 33:4-6). Yes, the Holy Spirit, the breath of God, acted as the Divine Executive in the creation.

2. He Was Involved in the Writing of the Scriptures

The place of the Holy Spirit as the administrative Author of the Scriptures is clearly manifest. David declares of his own writings, "The Spirit of the Lord was upon me, and his word was on my tongue" (2 Sam. 23:2). The prophets openly acknowledge His authorship. Micah (3:8) declares, "Truly I am full of power by the spirit of the Lord, and of judgment, and of might, to declare unto Jacob his transgression, and to Israel his sin." Ezekiel (2:2) confesses, "The spirit entered into me when he spake unto me, and set me upon my feet, that I heard him that spake unto me." Indeed, he becomes quite dramatic in identifying the active ministry of the Spirit in his writing.

> In the sixth year, in the sixth month on the fifth day, while I was sitting in my house and the elders of Judah were sitting before me, the hand of the Sovereign Lord came upon me there. . . . He stretched out what looked like a hand and took me by the hair of my head. The Spirit lifted me up between earth and heaven and in visions of God he took me to Jerusalem . . . And there before me was the glory of the God of Israel (Ezek. 8:1-4, NIV).

It may well have been from the significance of this imagery that Peter many years later declared (2 Pet. 1:20-21): "The prophecy came not in old time by the will of man: but holy men of God spake as they were moved by the Holy Ghost." The word "moved" is a verb of active conveyance, and is the same as used in John 2:8 and translated there as "bear." "He saith to them, Draw out now and bear unto the governor of the feast." The writers of the Scriptures are borne along by the Holy Spirit.

The symbol of the Spirit as the breath of God is revived in the well-known statement of 2 Tim. 3:16: "All Scripture is God-breathed and is useful for teaching, rebuking, correcting and training in righteousness, so that the man of God may be thoroughly equipped for every good work" (NIV).

Even the very wording of Scripture, the vocabulary from which Paul drew in writing, is identified in 1 Cor. 2:4-16. We quote from the NASB: "My message and my preaching were not in persuasive words of wisdom, but in demonstration of the Spirit and of power, that your faith should not rest on the wisdom of men, but on the power of God." Then, changing to the editorial "we" he continues:

> Yet we do speak wisdom among those who are mature . . . the wisdom which none of the rulers of this age has understood; for if they had understood it, they would not have crucified the Lord of glory; but just as it is written,
> "THINGS WHICH EYE HAS NOT SEEN AND EAR HAS
> NOT HEARD,
> AND WHICH HAVE NOT ENTERED THE HEART OF MAN,
> ALL THAT GOD HAS PREPARED FOR THOSE WHO
> LOVE HIM."

Paul then continues his witness:

> To us God revealed them through the Spirit; for the Spirit searches all things, even the depths of God. For who among men knows the thoughts of a man except the spirit of the man, which is in him? Even so the thoughts of God no one knows except the Spirit of God. Now we have received, not the spirit of the world, but the Spirit who is from God, that we might know the things freely given to us by God, which things we also speak, not in words taught by human wisdom, but in those taught by the Spirit, combining spiritual thoughts with spiritual words.

Thus Paul identifies the very words he uses in expressing things of God with the vocabulary learned from the Holy Spirit—"Not in words taught by human wisdom, but in those taught by the Spirit." And, in this learning, Paul was rich. His vocabulary makes a fascinating study.

3. The Holy Spirit Was Active in the Life of Jesus

In relation to Christ, the Holy Spirit was the executive for God the Father.

This was true from the very incarnation. The word "incarnation" is from the Greek *carnis*, "flesh," and is defined as a clothing or state of being clothed with flesh. It was the union of Divinity with humanity which was uniquely accomplished in Christ. It is most delicately expressed by the physician, Luke, as he reports Mary's conversation with the angel Gabriel. "The angel answered, 'The Holy Spirit will come upon you, and the power of the Most High will overshadow you. So the holy one to be born will be called the Son of God' " (Luke 1:35, NIV).

This, of course, was later confirmed to Joseph as reported by Matthew, with the added information, "All this took place to fulfill what the Lord had said through the prophet: 'The virgin will be with child and will give birth to a son, and they will call him Immanuel'—which means, 'God with us' " (Matt. 1:22-23, NIV).

The Holy Spirit again was God's administrative agent at the time of Christ's baptism. Luke 3:21-22 records it: "When all the people were baptized, it came to pass, that Jesus also being baptized, and praying, the heaven was opened, and the Holy Ghost descended in a bodily shape like a dove upon him, and a voice came from heaven which said, Thou art my beloved Son: in thee I am well pleased." This, of course, had been foreseen by Isaiah who expressed it twice, in 11:1-2 and 42:1. "There shall come forth a rod out of the stem of Jesse, and a Branch shall grow out of his roots: and the spirit of the Lord shall rest upon him, the spirit of wisdom and understanding, the spirit of counsel and might, the spirit of knowledge and of fear of the Lord," and "Behold my servant, whom I uphold; mine elect, in whom my soul delighteth; I have put my spirit upon him: he shall bring forth judgment to the Gentiles."

Interestingly, the Holy Spirit was instrumental in our Lord's temptation, in that Luke records: "Jesus being full of the Holy Ghost returned from Jordan, and was led by the Spirit into the wilderness, being forty days tempted of the devil. And in those days he did eat nothing: and when they were ended, he afterward hungered" (Luke 4:1-2). He who taught us to pray, "Lead us not into temptation," was himself "led by the Spirit," to be tempted. Mark (1:12) says dramatically, "The Spirit driveth him." He was literally catapulted by the Spirit into the temptation.

How could this be? There certainly must have been reason for this. Jamieson, Fausset, and Brown in their *Commentary on the Whole Bible*, present a reasonable set of answers.

> First, we judge, to give our Lord a taste of what lay before Him in the work He had undertaken; next, to make a trial of the glorious furniture for it which He had just received; further, to give Him encouragement by the victory now to be won to go forward, spoiling principalities and powers until at length He should make a show of them openly, triumphing over them in His cross; again, that the tempter, too, might get a taste, at the very outset, of the new kind of material in *man* which he would find he had here to deal with; finally, and most important, that He might acquire experimentally ability "to succor them that are tempted" (Heb. 2:18).[1]

The very ministry of our Lord was saturated with the

Holy Spirit. It was in the power of the Spirit that He cast out demons (Matt. 12:28); that He taught (Luke 4:14-15); that He carried out a quiet, tender, spiritual ministry to the Gentiles: "Behold my servant, whom I have chosen; my beloved, in whom my soul is well pleased: I will put my spirit upon him, and he shall shew judgment to the Gentiles. He shall not strive, nor cry; neither shall any man hear his voice in the streets. A bruised reed shall he not break, and smoking flax shall he not quench, till he send forth judgment unto victory. And in his name shall the Gentiles trust" (Matt. 12:18-21).

4. The Holy Spirit and the Atonement

In a most sensitive area, the Holy Spirit is the Divine Executive in the matter of man's redemption. Indeed, this most important provision occupies the attention of *all Members* of the Godhead.

a. God the Father *planned* it. Paul declared, "This is good and acceptable in the sight of God our Saviour; who will have all men to be saved, and to come unto the knowledge of the truth" (1 Tim. 2:3-4). Peter also announces this: "The Lord is not slack concerning his promise, as some men count slackness; but is longsuffering to us-ward, not willing that any should perish, but that all should come to repentance" (2 Pet. 3:9). The foundation for this plan was indeed voiced by God to Satan immediately after man's fall, when God declared to him: "I will put enmity between you and the woman, and between your seed and her seed; He shall bruise you on the head, and you shall bruise him on the heel" (Gen. 3:15, NASB). From the very day of man's Fall God set forth a divine plan for man's redemption.

b. God the Son *purchased* it. "There is one God, and one mediator between God and men, the man Christ Jesus; who gave himself a ransom for all, to be testified in due time" (1 Tim. 2:5-6). "When we were without strength, in due time Christ died for the ungodly. . . . God commendeth his love toward us, in that, while we were yet sinners, Christ died for us" (Rom. 5:6-8).

The witness of the Scriptures in Hebrews is most enlightening on Christ's *presenting His body* as a sacrifice for sin.

> It is impossible for the blood of bulls and goats to take away sins. Therefore, when He comes into the world, He says, "SACRIFICE AND OFFERING THOU HAST NOT DESIRED, BUT A BODY THOU HAST PREPARED FOR ME; IN WHOLE BURNT OFFERINGS AND SACRIFICES FOR SIN THOU HAST TAKEN NO PLEASURE. THEN I SAID, 'BEHOLD, I HAVE COME (IN THE ROLL OF THE BOOK IT IS WRITTEN OF ME) TO DO THY WILL, O GOD.' " After saying above, "SACRIFICES AND OFFERINGS AND WHOLE BURNT OFFERINGS AND SACRIFICES FOR SIN THOU HAST NOT DESIRED, NOR HAST THOU TAKEN PLEASURE IN THEM" (which are offered according to the Law), then He said, "BEHOLD I HAVE COME TO DO THY WILL." He takes away the first in order to establish the second. By this will we have been sanctified through the offering of the body of Jesus Christ once for all (Heb. 10:4-10, NASB).

Christ took the body God gave Him and willingly yielded it up for the sacrifice of death on the Cross in obedience to what He knew God willed for the redemption of men.

c. It is God the Holy Spirit who *administers* the plan of salvation.

(1) He woos the sinner. Revelation 22:17 declares: "The Spirit and the bride say, Come. And let him that heareth say, Come. And let him that is athirst come. And whosoever will, let him take the water of life freely." The invitation comes from Him. The Church reinforces and announces it.

(2) He awakens the sinner's sleeping conscience. "He, when He comes," declared Jesus, "will convict the

world concerning sin, and righteousness, and judgment" (John 16:8, NASB).

(3) He is then the administrative agent for the four aspects of salvation.

(a) He brings *justification* with its forgiveness of sins. "Ye are justified in the name of the Lord Jesus, and by the Spirit of our God" (1 Cor. 6:11).

(b) He is the agent for *regeneration* with its new birth and life eternal. "That which is born of the flesh is flesh; and that which is born of the Spirit is spirit" (John 3:3-8; cf. Titus 3:5).

(c) He is also the agent for *adoption*—for man's being accepted into the family of God with its privileges and responsibilities. "Because ye are sons, God hath sent forth the Spirit of his Son into your hearts, crying, Abba, Father. Therefore thou art no more a servant, but a son; and if a son, then an heir of God through Christ" (Gal. 4:6-7). What a prospect! And, finally,

(d) He is the administrative agent of the Godhead for man's *sanctification*. "God hath from the beginning chosen you to salvation through sanctification of the Spirit and belief of the truth" (2 Thess. 2:13).

5. Sanctification and the Atonement

Now sanctification itself is an integral part of the atonement, and also a product of the Trinity. God the Father *planned* it. It was no afterthought by God. "He chose us in him before the creation of the world to be holy and blameless in his sight" (Eph. 1:4, NIV). God had nothing less than this in mind when He created man in His image.

There can be no surprise, then, that Christ *purchased* it. "Christ also loved the church, and gave himself for it; that he might sanctify and cleanse it with the washing of water by the word" (Eph. 5:22-26). He loved not only the sinful world (John 3:16), but also the believing Church. "Wherefore Jesus also, that he might sanctify the people with his own blood, suffered without the gate" (Heb. 13:12).

The Holy Spirit carries through God's plan as He *administers* sanctification among His people.

Sanctification carries the definition, "to make sacred or holy; to free from sin; to purify; to make Christlike." It involves the negative of cleansing and deliverance, and the positive of imparted goodness, godliness, and developing Christian maturity. Conversion is becoming *a Christian*—the noun. Sanctification is becoming *Christian*—the adjective.

Sanctification has three aspects, all under the administration of the Holy Spirit.

a. Initial sanctification is that cleansing of the outward sins of acquired depravity, largely the sins of the flesh, which we usually term "being saved from" certain sins. However, this can correctly be termed initial sanctification. Writing to the unspiritual, carnal Corinthian church (see 1 Cor. 3:1-4), Paul says in the same letter, 6:9-11 (NIV):

> Do you not know that the wicked will not inherit the kingdom of God? Do not be deceived: Neither the sexually immoral nor idolaters nor adulterers nor male prostitutes nor homosexual offenders nor thieves nor the greedy nor drunkards nor slanderers nor swindlers will inherit the kingdom of God. And that is what some of you were. But you were washed, you were sanctified, you were justified in the name of the Lord Jesus Christ and by the Spirit of our God (see also 1:2).

This is accomplished for the sinner by the *presence* of the Holy Spirit in the experience of conversion.

b. Entire sanctification is that complete, crisis experience following conversion, dealing with the inherited, sinful nature, with sins of the spirit related to inherited depravity. It leaves no part of the personality untouched.

This is succinctly expressed to the well-saved church in Thessalonica: "The very God of peace sanctify you wholly; and I pray God your whole spirit and soul and body be preserved blameless unto the coming of our Lord Jesus Christ." Then Paul adds, "Faithful is he that calleth you, who also will do it" (1 Thess. 5:23-24). This is accomplished in the believer by the *baptism* of the Holy Spirit in the experience of entire sanctification (Acts 11:15-17; 15:8-9).

c. Progressive sanctification is that growth, renewal, maturing, holy living, continual cleansing which should be the unfolding life of every believer, but especially of those who are Spirit-filled. It is typified by Paul's statement given in 2 Cor. 3:18: "We all, with unveiled face beholding as in a mirror the glory of the Lord, are being transformed into the same image from glory to glory, just as from the Lord, the Spirit" (NASB). This is accomplished by the *abiding fullness* of the Holy Spirit in the life of the believer. The poet has caught something of this in the chorus:

> *Silently now I wait for Thee,*
> *Ready, my God, Thy will to see,*
> *Open mine eyes, illumine me,*
> *Spirit divine.*

6. The Paraclete on Duty

Christ had identified the Holy Spirit as the Paraclete, the One who could be called alongside to perform many and varied ministries.

His guidance as recorded for the Early Church is noteworthy, and is available today. There is the case of Philip. Acts 8 tells the story.

> The angel of the Lord spake unto Philip, saying, Arise, and go toward the south unto the way that goeth down from Jerusalem unto Gaza, which is desert. And

he arose and went: and, behold, a man of Ethiopia, an eunuch of great authority under Candace queen of the Ethiopians, who had the charge of all her treasure, and had come to Jerusalem for to worship, was returning, and sitting in his chariot read Esaias the prophet. Then the Spirit said unto Philip, Go near, and join thyself to this chariot. . . . And when they were come up out of the water, the Spirit of the Lord caught away Philip, that the eunuch saw him no more: and he went on his way rejoicing (vv. 26-29, 39.)

Then there were Barnabas and Saul. "As they ministered to the Lord and fasted, the Holy Ghost said, Separate me Barnabas and Saul for the work whereunto I have called them. . . . So they, being sent forth by the Holy Ghost, departed unto Seleucia" (Acts 13:2-4). And again, "When they had gone throughout Phrygia and the region of Galatia, and were forbidden of the Holy Ghost to preach the word in Asia, after they were come to Mysia, they assayed to go into Bithynia: but the Spirit suffered them not" (Acts 16:6-7). Sometimes the Spirit said yes, sometimes no.

The Spirit is a Guide for divine worship. Paul witnessed, "We are the true circumcision, who worship in the Spirit of God" (Phil. 3:3, NASB; see also John 4:20-24).

He also sets the standard for personal conduct. Paul, in Eph. 5:18-20, says: "Be filled with the Spirit; speaking to yourselves in psalms and hymns and spiritual songs, singing and making melody in your heart to the Lord; giving thanks always for all things unto God and the Father in the name of our Lord Jesus Christ; submitting yourselves one to another in the fear of God."

We are painfully conscious of our human limitations, especially in the area of prayer. How can we pray according to the will of God? Call alongside that divine Administrator of the Godhead, the Holy Spirit. Paul assures us, "The Spirit helps us in our weakness ... the Spirit himself intercedes for us with groans that words cannot express" (Rom. 8:26, NIV).

Indeed, in so many practical and pressing areas, the Paraclete is "on call" to be our Comforter, Helper, Teacher. He would carry out in our lives God's will for us.

7. The Unpardonable Sin

There is a sin which Jesus said is unforgivable—the sin against the Holy Spirit. The particular occasion of Christ's announcement regarding this unpardonable sin was when the Pharisees would have given credit to Satan for the deliverance of a demon-possessed man. "This man casts out demons only by Beelzebub the ruler of the demons" (Matt. 12:24, NASB), they declared. Deeply disturbed, Jesus summarizes His reply by the harsh statement: "I say to you, any sin and blasphemy shall be forgiven men, but blasphemy against the Spirit shall not be forgiven. And whoever shall speak a word against the Son of Man, it shall be forgiven him; but whoever shall speak against the Holy Spirit, it shall not be forgiven him, either in this age, or in the age to come" (Matt. 12:31-32, NASB).

Jesus is here defending the utterly essential administrative work of the Holy Spirit, whether it be in the casting out of evil spirits, or the forgiveness of sins, or the cleansing of the heart. The Holy Spirit is indispensable, and God depends on the reliable, effectual work of the Spirit to carry through His plans for mankind. Whoever discards the Holy Spirit discards hopes of God's work being done in his heart. It is an unforgivable sin.

However, it must be added that the unpardonable sin is more an attitude than a single act. As long as one persists in it he has no pardon. But forgiveness is immediately available, as for any sin, if this attitude is discarded.

He who fears lest he has committed such a sin has not. His concern prohibits that possibility.

The very existence of such a hopeless possibility emphasizes the importance of the Holy Spirit in the affairs of man. It calls for a renewed respect toward Him and a constant renewal of His presence in the heart.

8. The Holy Spirit and the Church

a. The Holy Spirit Is the Agent Through Whom God Established the Church

Paul writes to the people of Ephesus as those who are representative of the Gentile believers. Such would hold equal rights with Jewish believers as members of the Church. With God there is no favoritism under the new dispensation. This became a glorious "bill of rights" to all the Gentile world.

> Remember that formerly you who are Gentiles by birth and called "uncircumcised" by those who call themselves "the circumcision" (that done in the body by the hands of men)—remember that at that time you were separate from Christ, excluded from citizenship in Israel and foreigners to the covenants of the promise, without hope and without God in the world. But now in Christ Jesus you who once were far away have been brought near through the blood of Christ.
>
> For he himself is our peace, who has made the two one and has destroyed the barrier, the dividing wall of hostility. . . . He came and preached peace to you who were far away and peace to those who were near. For through him we both have access to the Father by one Spirit.
>
> Consequently, you are no longer foreigners and aliens, but fellow citizens with God's people and members of God's household, built on the foundation of the apostles and prophets, with Christ Jesus himself as the chief cornerstone. In him the whole building is joined together and rises to become a holy temple in

41

the Lord. And in him you too are being built together to become a dwelling in which God lives by his Spirit (Eph. 2:11-14, 19-22, NIV).

Through the merits of His cross Christ preached peace both "to you [Gentiles] who were far away" and "to those [Jews] who were near." As Charles W. Carter expresses it:

> Before Christ the Jews had access to God by means of the shadows and types that the law afforded. The Gentiles could have access to God only by becoming proselytes, which meant that they had to become Jews in religion. Thus only Jews had access to God. Now, however, Jewish and Gentile believers in Christ have a common, free access to God through His Holy Spirit (Acts 2:21, 38-39). Here the doctrine of the Holy Trinity comes into clear revelation. Believers have access to God the Father in the peace provided by the cross of His Son through the agency and operation of the Holy Spirit.[2]

Paul has used three symbols to show the common relationship Christians have to one another in Christ. They are "fellow citizens," they have become "a holy temple," they are now "a dwelling in which God lives." What a unifying gospel to preach today, to all people of all races!

It would be in the confidence of this that Sabine Baring-Gould wrote:

> Like a mighty army
>   Moves the church of God;
> Brothers, we are treading
>   Where the saints have trod.
> We are not divided,
>   All one body we,
> One in hope, in doctrine,
>   One in charity.

b. The Holy Spirit Is the Bond Holding the Church Together

Paul proclaims in the same Epistle: "Make every effort to keep the unity of the Spirit through the bond of peace. There is one body and one Spirit—just as you were called to one hope when you were called—one Lord, one faith, one baptism; one God and Father of all, who is over all and through all and in all" (Eph. 4:3-6, NIV).

The unspiritual Corinthian church is the unhappy example of a divisive, contentious church, while the Spirit-filled church at Jerusalem (Acts 2:41-47) was a happy example of a unified, growing church. Note the description of that joyous group:

> Those who accepted his message were baptized, and about three thousand were added to their number that day. They devoted themselves to the apostles' teaching and to the fellowship, to the breaking of bread and to prayer. Everyone was filled with awe, and many wonders and miraculous signs were done by the apostles. All the believers were together and had everything in common. Selling their possessions and goods, they gave to anyone as he had need. Every day they continued to meet together in the temple courts. They broke bread in their homes and ate together with glad and sincere hearts, praising God and enjoying the favor of all the people. And the Lord added to their number daily those who were being saved (NIV).

What a tribute to the "unity of the Spirit"!

Probably 1 Cor. 12:13 is the premier verse related to such unity: "By one Spirit are we all baptized into one body, whether we be bond or free; and have been all made to drink into one Spirit." (But see also Gal. 3:27-28.)

c. The Holy Spirit Is the Distributor of Gifts to the Church

The subject of gifts will be discussed at length in the

43

next chapter. It will be well at this point, however, to observe that there are three approaches to the presence and working of the Holy Spirit in the life of the believer.

(1) The Calvinistic view is that, at conversion, the Christian receives the baptism of the Holy Spirit and may be continuously filled with Him in a normal Christian life, but that there is no subsequent Spirit baptism or sanctification as a crisis experience to be anticipated after conversion. These are merely ongoing, growth experiences.

(2) The Pentecostal and the charismatic sees such a post-conversion baptism with the Spirit as a promised, attainable experience, with signs, healings, and tongues as the chief evidences of such a crisis experience.

(3) The Wesleyan finds in the Scripture the promise of and the exhortation to a personal, crisis filling with the Spirit subsequent to, and usually distinct from conversion, as a part of the plan of atonement, bringing a defined experience of cleansing and empowering known scripturally as Entire Sanctification, and promising, as a normal spiritual life, a constant refilling with the Spirit, a life of consistent victory over sin and a steady spiritual growth.

The following pages will be dedicated to supporting this third viewpoint, which we believe to have been eternally conceived in the purpose of God, to be both scriptural and experiential, and to have been continuously available and applicable through the centuries since Calvary.

4/

THE FRUIT AND THE GIFTS
OF THE SPIRIT

I. The Fruit of the Spirit

The Holy Spirit in the life of the believer bears fruit. This fruit of the Spirit is the development in the individual of God's characteristics flowing from the divine nature. Spiritual character is its offspring. It is directly related to the abiding presence of the Spirit.

Let us examine this fruitfulness in three passages.

1. Love

Galatians 5:22-23 lists as "fruit of the Spirit" some nine qualities which are characteristic of Christlikeness in its richest expression: "The fruit of the Spirit is love, joy, peace, longsuffering, gentleness, goodness, faith, meekness, temperance." In contrast are the works of the flesh: "Adultery, fornication, uncleanness, lasciviousness, idolatry, witchcraft, hatred, variance, emulations, wrath, strife, seditions, heresies, envyings, murders, drunkenness, revellings, and such like" (vv. 19-21). To move from one to the other is to go from the harshness of the workshop to the fragrance of the garden. The one indeed is works, the other fruit.

Since in this verse "fruit" is in the singular, there are those, such as G. Campbell Morgan, who claim "love" to be the one fruit of the Spirit, with the qualities of that Christian love listed in the eight following aspects. This may be so. On the other hand, the nine may well be looked at as one indivisible fruit cluster, with many flavors and colors, the chief characteristic being that of love.

Like fruit in the garden, this fruit develops slowly but constantly through the measured period of its life, coming to its peak of perfection in the stage of maturity. The sun, the darkness, the rain, and the breezes all make their contribution. But the chief nourishment for its development comes from the tree, the plant, or the vine which produces it. Characteristically, the fruit is attractive in its coloring, its form, its scent. It is tasty and nourishing to one devouring it. And, possibly of greatest importance, it carries within itself the seed of reproduction for the necessary purpose of propagation.

2. The True Vine

Without specifically mentioning the Holy Spirit, the Bible presents the concept of fruit in Jesus' parable of the "true vine," recorded in John 15. The fruitful branch is "purged" that it might bring forth more fruit; the unfruitful branch is removed and destroyed. But the particular requirement for fruitfulness is simply "abiding" in the vine. Particular "glory" accrues to the husbandman (the Father) from the branches which bear much fruit. "Ye," the branches, after close observation of your response to the opportunities, to the incalculable privileges of being a branch, are chosen, pruned, and nourished that you might bring forth fruit which shall remain—even after the branch has perished. Thus the aspect of fruit here emphasized would seem to be that of the seeds of reproduction which remain for the propagation of the faith.

3. The Planted Seed

Fruit is again the subject of John 12:23-25. The final days of His life were approaching and Jesus looked upon them with awe, but also with confidence.

> Jesus answered them, saying, The hour is come, that the Son of man should be glorified. Verily, verily, I say unto you, Except a corn of wheat fall into the ground and die, it abideth alone: but if it die, it bringeth forth much fruit. He that loveth his life shall lose it; and he that hateth his life in this world shall keep it unto life eternal.

In order to bear "much fruit" Jesus, as a corn of wheat—or more exactly "the" corn of wheat—must be "glorified," must "fall into the ground and die." From His death and resurrection would the "much fruit" of His life be established. The believer likewise, in order to bear much fruit, must "lose his life," or he will "abide alone," that is, die without bearing fruit.

In order to share this fruitfulness with their Lord, "believers must do more than associate themselves with Calvary as those who look upon the Sin-bearer who suffers there *for* them. They are called to identify themselves with Him *on* the Cross, as being crucified *with* Him and fully united with Him, and He with them so that His death means the death of their old nature, leading to a new life in the power of the Resurrection."[1] (See Rom. 6:4, 6.)

This is what Paul means when he declares, "If we be dead with Christ, we believe that we shall also live with him: knowing that Christ being raised from the dead dieth no more; death hath no more dominion over him. For in that he died, he died unto sin once: but in that he liveth, he liveth unto God. Likewise, reckon ye also yourselves to be *dead indeed unto sin,* but *alive unto God* through Jesus Christ our Lord" (Rom. 6:8-11). He then continues in v. 22, "Now being made free from sin, and become servants to God, ye have your fruit unto holiness, and the end everlasting life." This aspect of fruitfulness emphasizes the cost, as well as the reward.

It is in this light that Paul testifies, "I am crucified with Christ: nevertheless I live; yet not I, but Christ liveth in me: and the life which I now live in the flesh I live by the faith of the Son of God, who loved me, and gave himself for me" (Gal. 2:20). Through a positive decision on the part of the believer, the old sinful self has been "denied," "crucified" (Matt. 16:24-25). The believer is dead unto sin. Paul expressed this in the perfect tense of "I am crucified," the tense which identifies that which happened at a point of time, and which continues as a life pattern which he must constantly affirm.

Through sharing this experience of crucifixion on the Cross with his Lord, the believer will also share in "bringing forth much fruit." This fruit will be that of personal holiness in exhibiting the manifold fruit of the Spirit, and also that of reproduction, of being used of God to the winning of many precious souls unto Him.

Be it noted that every one of these passages on fruit is expected from every child of God. And, in a large measure, godliness is measured by fruitfulness.

H. Orton Wiley observes that the fruit of the Spirit is

the communication to the individual of the graces flowing from the divine nature, and has its issue in character rather than in qualifications for service. It is the overflow of the divine life which follows as a necessary consequence of the Spirit's abiding presence. Fruit grows by cultivation, from the Spirit's abiding presence. Fruit is not of man's producing, it grows by the life that is in the Vine.[2]

II. The Gifts of the Spirit

In the popular conception, gifts of the Spirit have become related to the charismatic movement. To clarify the word, let us note the following:

1. All Christians Are Charismatic

The heart of the Greek word for gift is *charis* (grace). For example, Rom. 6:23 states, "The gift [charisma] of God is eternal life." Thus *charismata* is the plural of gifts "involving grace on the part of God as the Donor," according to W. E. Vine.[3] The two, *grace* and *gift,* are tied together in Rom. 5:15, "The *free gift* is not like the transgression. For if by the transgression of the one the many died, much more did the *grace* of God . . . abound to the many" (NASB).

In the light of this, the dictionary definition of *charisma* is unfortunate. "*Charisma* 1. *Theol.* An extraordinary spiritual gift or grace granted to individuals for the benefit of others, as the power to heal, etc." (Funk and Wagnalls). Now "charisma" may well *include* this. However, the *primary* meaning remains—a gift by God's grace which brings to man eternal life. Furthermore the illustration in the dictionary is unfortunate. As will later be noted, "the power to heal" is not the first or the most important gift, but rather the fifth of nine when the gifts are listed in order of importance in 1 Cor. 12:28-30.

2. Every Christian Is a "Gifted" Christian

God leaves none of His children without at least one gift. Paul is clear on this. To the Corinthians he declares: "The manifestation of the Spirit is given to every man to profit withal" (1 Cor. 12:7); to the Ephesians: "Unto every one of us is given grace according to the measure of the gift of Christ" (Eph. 4:7); and to the Church in Rome: "As we have many members in one body . . . having then gifts differing according to the grace that is given to us" (Rom. 12:4-6). Thus every Christian has a responsibility. What a sad picture many a church presents—an overworked pastor and a few dedicated members, but a large majority of "pew-warming worshippers." This is not God's plan at all. In the Holy Spirit *all* the saints are to be equipped "for the work of service." There should be no "drones" in God's "hive."

3. Gift's Are Distributed According to the Spirit's Choice

Paul tells the Corinthian church, "There are diversities of gifts, but the same Spirit." And he proceeds to enumerate various gifts as given "to one . . . to another . . . to another . . . and to another . . . and to another . . . " This he concludes with, "But all these worketh that one and the selfsame Spirit, dividing to every man severally as he will" (1 Cor. 12:4, 8-11). Thus there will be found varying gifts distributed with a divine wisdom. There is variety within unity. Properly accepted and properly used these gifts can be invaluable within the Church in working out its purpose both for all its members and for the entire community. And every member should be respected for his God-given contribution, and none envied for his presumably superior gift.

4. The Inroads of Clericalism

Clericalism was one of the unhappy results of the

recognition of the Church by Constantine in the fourth century. In order to supply suitable and official representatives to the state, the church stimulated hierarchical development. Bishops, presbyters, and deacons, who had already in great measure gained supremacy over laymen, became more authoritative after the union with the state. Thus the clergy became the officials of the church, and a stratification was formed. They became the official voice of the church. In particular, the sacraments became the sole responsibility of the clergy. The layman's access to God was through the clergy. As a result the layman became a worshipper and not a participant in church activities. The majority of Christians became "unemployed." Indeed, the "charismatic movement" is in this sense, a protest against clericalism. The proper use of the gifts of the Spirit by His people is God's answer to this situation.

5. Gifts that Serve

Gifts are bestowed on believers as an endowment of useful service. Paul told the Corinthians that gifts were given "for the common good" (1 Cor. 12:7, NASB), and told the Ephesians that the purpose of their gifts was "for the perfecting of the saints, for the work of the ministry, for the edifying of the body of Christ" (Eph. 4:12).

Peter, out of a lifetime of experience and observation, declared *in the twilight of life:* "As each one has received a 'special gift' *(charisma)*, employ it in serving one another, as good stewards of the manifold grace of God" (1 Pet. 4:10, NASB).

Here is disclosed one of the very practical aspects of the working of the Holy Spirit in the heart of the believer. Through the Holy Spirit, God desires to put His saints to work "serving one another." Now this service is that of ministry—waiting upon, or caring for one another's needs. It suggests the giving of oneself for others in service, both spiritual and material.

It is that act of serving *(diakoneo)* of which Jesus said of himself "I am among you as the one who serves" (Luke 22:27, NASB). But see the context, starting with the 24th verse:

> There arose also a dispute among them as to which one of them was regarded to be the greatest. And He said to them, "The kings of the Gentiles lord it over them; and those who have authority over them are called 'Benefactors.' But not so with you, but let him who is the greatest among you become as the youngest, and the leader as the servant. For who is greater, the one who reclines at table, or the one who serves? Is it not the one who reclines at table? But I am among you as the one who serves (NASB).

Was not James speaking to the same subject when comparing faith with works?

> What good is it, my brothers, if a man claims to have faith but has not deeds? Can such faith save him? Suppose a brother or sister is without clothes and daily food. If one of you says to him, "Go, I wish you well; keep warm and well fed," but does nothing about his physical needs, what good is it? In the same way, faith by itself, if it is not accompanied by action, is dead (Jas. 2:14-17, NIV).

Yes, "special gifts" *(charismata)* granted by God to His children are a challenge to service, to usefulness, to practical Christian charity in its richest sense. It is not without significance that Jesus, himself, after being anointed by the Holy Spirit, "went about doing good." As Jesus said of himself, "The Spirit of the Lord is upon me, because he hath anointed me to preach the gospel to the poor; he hath sent me to heal the brokenhearted, to preach deliverance to the captives, and recovering of sight to the blind, to set at liberty them that are bruised, to preach the acceptable year of the Lord" (Luke 4:18-19). And it was Jesus who declared to His disciples, and to us, "As my Father hath sent me, even so send I you" (John 20:21).

This is charismatic Christianity at its best.

III. THE NATURE OF THE GIFTS OF THE SPIRIT

1. A Description of the Gifts

Gifts may be described as the varied manifestation of the Holy Spirit in the ever varying human personality, with no two exactly the same, differing largely according to the person's abilities and talents. It will be interesting, in the light of this, to examine the gifts which are listed in the Bible. These are centered in the three books of Romans, Ephesians, with two somewhat related lists in First Corinthians.

1 Cor. 12:28-30	1 Cor. 12:6-10	Rom. 12:3-8	Eph. 4:7, 11-16
1st Apostles			Apostles
2nd Prophets	Prophecy	Prophecy	Prophets
3rd Teachers		Teaching	Pastors and Teachers
"after that"	A word of wisdom A word of knowledge	Ministry (service)	Evangelists
Miracles	Miracles	Exhortation (encouragement)	
Healings	Healing	Giving (liberality)	
Helps	Discerning of spirits	Ruling (leading)	

53

1 Cor. 12:28-30	1 Cor. 12:6-10	Rom. 12:3-8	Eph. 4:7, 11-16
Governments	Faith	Showing mercy	
Diversities of tongues	Tongues		
Interpretation of tongues	Interpretation		

Note some facts about these lists. These gifts are discussed with only three churches, tongues with only one—in spite of the fact that they had previously been introduced to Ephesus. Only two gifts—prophecy and teaching—are listed in all. An important gift like evangelism is listed with only the one church, though certainly practiced in all. Because of the wide variations among the lists, it may well be doubted that this is a full accounting of all the gifts.

The order of importance is also significant. It should be noted, however, that some of the less spectacular gifts such as helps, ministry, and showing mercy are particularly related to the type of service called for by Peter, and should not be considered unimportant in God's sight. They were certainly practiced in all churches.

2. Gifts and Talents

Does our Lord's parable of the talents (Matt. 25:14-30) speak to this subject? W. E. Vine points out that "The talent (talanton), denoting something weighted, has provided the meaning of the English word as a gift or ability, especially under the influence of the Parable of the Talents." Further, a talent is defined in the dictionary as "a faculty or gift."[4]

In the light of this, note that Jesus spoke of the man "who called his own servants, and delivered unto them his goods . . . to every man according to his ability." Every man, then, was accountable for what he did with what he had received. To each who used his assets, the rewards were the same: "Well done, thou good and faithful servant . . . enter thou into the joy of thy lord." But for him who was unresponsive and irresponsible, there was the designation of "unprofitable," and the condemnation to outer darkness.

Surely this speaks clearly to the believer's responsibility for the using and improving of the gifts given him by the Spirit. The penalty of neglect is severe.

3. The Hazard of Gifts

With all their beneficial accomplishments and attractiveness, gifts also have their dangers. In a very intriguing fashion Paul, in the 12th chapter of 1 Corinthians, likens the Church to a body, with its various members related to the gifts each may exhibit. In that graphic figure he has also outlined to us risks which may be incurred.

Is there not the danger of independence and of jealousy among factions within the church as in Corinth?

> If the foot shall say, Because I am not the hand, I am not of the body; is it therefore not of the body? And if the ear shall say, Because I am not an eye, I am not of the body; is it therefore not of the body? If the whole body were an eye, where were the hearing? If the whole were hearing, where were the smelling? But now hath God set the members every one of them in the body, as it hath pleased him. And if they were all one member, where were the body? But now are they many members, yet but one body. And the eye cannot say to the hand, I have no need of thee: nor again the head to the feet, I have no need of you. Nay, much more those members of the body, which seem to be more feeble, are necessary (1 Cor. 12:15-22).

Can there not also be the danger of a feeling of superiority, as there was in Corinth? "Those members of the body, which we think to be less honourable, upon these we bestow more abundant honour; and our uncomely parts have more abundant comeliness. For our comely parts have no need: but God hath tempered the body together, having given more abundant honour to that part which lacked" (vv. 23-24).

Is there not, still further, the danger of divisiveness, which also appeared in the Corinthian church? Verses 25-27 declare: "That there should be no schism in the body; but that the members should have the same care one for another. And whether one member suffer, all the members suffer with it; or one member be honoured, all the members rejoice with it. Now ye are the body of Christ, and members in particular."

Commissioner Brengle used to give a vivid illustration of the meaning of unity in the body of Christ. "I am holding a nail between thumb and finger," he would illustrate, "and I am pounding the nail with a hammer held in the other hand. If I inadvertently miss the nail and hammer my thumb, I don't triumphantly stand aloof and say to that thumb, 'You had it coming to you, you clumsy thumb. Why don't you watch what you are doing? It's your fault.' " And he would mimic the attitude of delighted scorn.

"Oh no," he would say, seizing the thumb in the circling palm of the other hand and bringing it to his lips. "I comfort it; I soothe it; I caress it; I ease its pain. It has been hurt. It's part of me. . . . Yes, we're all parts of the body of Christ," he would conclude. "We must suffer together, and then we will rejoice together." Oh, the tragedy of divisiveness within the body of Christ.

Is there not the danger of reversing the order of importance, again as did the Corinthians? "God hath set some in the church, first apostles, secondarily prophets, thirdly teachers, after that miracles, then gifts of healings, helps, governments, diversities of tongues" (v. 28).

And "tongues," the last and least of the gifts, can precipitate each of these dangers—the dangers of independence and jealousy, of feelings of superiority, of divisiveness, of laying claim to being the most important of the gifts. Those who practice tongues will deny this. However, in the final instance tongues appears to them to be the most important "sign," the greatest gift of all, the evidence of their being favored above others by the Spirit in His distribution.

And particularly there is the danger of identifying any one (or even all) of the gifts as *the* evidence of the baptism with the Holy Spirit, or as a sign of His fulness, of His anointing (as do many of the charismatics). It is there we must part company. For *no one of the gifts is available to all believers.* First Corinthians 12:8-11 says, "To one . . . to another . . . as he wills." Furthermore, into each of the questions of vv. 30 and 31 there is built in the Greek a "no" *(mē)*, not translated in the KJV but properly included in the NASB, which reads: "All are not apostles, are they? All are not prophets, are they? All are not teachers, are they? All are not workers of miracles, are they? All do not have gifts of healing, do they? All do not speak with tongues, do they? All do not interpret, do they?"

Indeed, individually or collectively *these gifts are not a measure of the true spirituality* of the person, or of the gift of the Holy Spirit. Consider the unspiritual nature of the Corinthian church which "came behind in no gift."

Then we must ask questions. What relation *do* "gifts" have to godliness? to holiness? to an outpouring of the Holy Spirit? to the fullness of the Spirit? Indeed, do gifts always accompany the baptism, the fullness of the Holy Spirit? In considering Corinthian Christians alone it is questionable, for we find them rich in their gifts (1 Cor. 1:7) but poverty stricken in the Spirit (3:1). Actually there is no record that the Corinthians had *ever* been filled with the Spirit. Certainly they were not Spirit-filled then.

In the New Testament record in Acts of some 10 occasions of the infusion of the Holy Spirit on believers, "tongues" is mentioned with only three of them, (2:1-4; 10:46; 19:6), "prophecy" with but one (19:6), and other gifts only implied, not specified. Obviously, then, the receipt of gifts, per se, is not *the* sign of such a baptism, such a fullness.

4. Gifts, Fruit, and Ministries of the Holy Spirit Compared

There are three aspects of the Spirit's relationship to the believer—the ministries, the fruit, and the gifts.

In His *ministries* as the administrator of the Godhead, the Holy Spirit brings the believer into repentance, into a saving faith of justification, regeneration, adoption, and sanctification. These ministries, of course, are an essential part of God's plan of redemption for mankind. Without them, God's saving grace would be unavailable. A rejection of the Spirit in His ministries is unpardonable. On the other hand, all of them are available to every member of the race of mankind.

The *fruit* of the Spirit is the harvest, marking growth and maturity. It produces ethical character. It is the true measure of holiness of life and practice in the believer. Every believer is expected to bear fruit. Fruit marks the unity of the Church in that it is common to all.

Gifts of the Spirit are basically God-given skills which are a ministry to others, which produce edification for the church and witness and evangelism to the unsaved. Gifts mark diversity, for they are given differently to each man, according to God's sovereign choice through the Spirit. Gifts properly used, keep the Christian useful. But gifts vary with the individual. No believer possesses them all. And no gift is available to every believer.

How wise and providential is God in providing man with these three aspects of the Spirit's relationship to him as a believer! How foolish man can be in allowing these to assume improper perspective one to another. Each must be cherished for its purpose and value.

The ministries and the fruit are essential, and available to every man. How illogical to make gifts more important than they. And, since gifts can more easily be counted for "credit," and are often dramatic, exciting, and spectacular, this can very easily be done.

Here is a mark of contrast between the Wesleyan holiness viewpoint and that of the charismatics. The emphasis of the former is upon ethical holiness, on purification, on the quiet, perfecting work of the Spirit baptism and on the cultivation of fruit unto holiness, all of which are available and expected by God in all believers. In contrast, the charismatic emphasis is upon the emotional, the ecstatic, the power of the supernatural, the physical manifestations, the exciting, the dramatic gifts of the Spirit, all of which are restricted to those whom the Spirit may choose. Let us give heed to Paul when he says, "I show you a more excellent way."

5/

THE CHARISMATIC RENEWAL

About the middle of the 20th century a new group of Pentecostals made their appearance. They shared the Pentecostal enthusiasm for a second blessing through a baptism "in" the Holy Spirit, with the manifestation of speaking in tongues. These are persons both within and outside the regular Pentecostal denominations. Among them are Protestants of various denominations, but also Roman Catholics. The charismatic community constitutes largely those who protest against formalism, ritualism, coldness, and sacramentalism, and who find their main release in the use of tongues and in miracles.

This Neo-Pentecostal movement gradually and increasingly has assumed the description of "charismatic."

To a large extent this has escaped the derogatory significance attached by many to "Pentecostal," and has helped the movement into an acceptance by a wide band of people of diverse denominations and doctrines. It carries a biblical connotation, popularized in the secular world, without the frenzy sometimes associated with Pentecostalism.

The so-called Charismatic Renewal has been propagated by various means. The Full Gospel Business Men's Fellowship International (FGBMFI), founded in 1953 in Los Angeles, has been in the forefront. Adopting the practice of holding breakfasts for Christian laymen, especially of the Full Gospel or Pentecostal leaning, the new movement began also to draw Christians of other churches, and not infrequently, pastors. Gifted speakers, attractive hotel surroundings, well-chosen music, dramatic testimonies helped weld together an important group across the country, and around the world. They continue in strength.

In fairness, the first word regarding the charismatic movement must be one of commendation, for it has been a meaningful force for God and righteousness in our day. With strong, evangelistic overtones the name of Jesus is being exalted, the gospel is being preached over the air in the extensive television and radio ministries, an aggressive worldwide outreach for Christ is being carried on, and many souls are being won for the Kingdom. Devoted people are finding Christian activity in witnessing for Christ, in counselling inquiring seekers, in being soul winners themselves, while their leaders give of themselves unsparingly to the task of spreading the gospel of Jesus Christ.

However, against these undeniable assets there must be measured equally undeniable liabilities. As we shall see, the doctrinal foundations of the movement do not stand up when tested against the Scriptures. Its priorities must be examined. And are those outward manifestations really scriptural?

The charismatic movement, while giving heed to most of the gifts, gives special attention to tongues and to healings, and also to the imminent return of Christ. We consider these in that order.

1. Tongues in the Scripture

In most instances, when the Word speaks of an infilling of the Holy Spirit it makes no reference to tongues. For example, Joel, in predicting the outpouring of the Spirit speaks of prophecy, dreams, and visions, but not "tongues" (Joel 2:28-32, Acts 2:17-21). When Isaiah predicts the outpouring of the Holy Spirit on the Messiah to come (Isa. 61:1-4, Luke 4:18-19), he says nothing about "tongues," and "tongues" were not given to Jesus when that prediction was fulfilled. The Spirit came mightily upon Zacharias (Luke 1:67-68), upon John the Baptist (Luke 1:15), upon Mary (Luke 1:35), upon Elizabeth (Luke 1:41), upon Simeon (Luke 2:25), but to none of them was given any gift of "tongues."

John the Baptist (Matt. 3:11), spoke of the baptism with the Holy Spirit, as did Jesus in Acts 1:5, but neither mentioned speaking with "tongues." The disciples received the Great Commission as variously recorded in Matt. 28:19-20, Luke 24:46-49 and John 20:21-23 without any mention of "tongues." The Holy Spirit came in a precise and full way a number of times in the Early Church, but only three times did they speak in any kind of "tongues."

Tongues *are* mentioned in some six places in the King James translation.

Isaiah's lament to Israel (28:11-12) "With stammering lips and another tongue will he speak to this people . . . yet they would not hear" is quoted by Paul in 1 Cor. 14:21. But far from supporting the use of tongues, Paul is pointing out that, just as words spoken in a strange language by a hostile nation did not lead the Hebrews to obedience, so speaking in strange, foreign languages will not profit the Corinthians.

Mark quotes Jesus as saying, "They shall speak with new tongues" (16:17-18). Several things need to be noted here. The total passage from vv. 9 through 20 is from unreliable manuscripts, as noted by NASB, NIV, NEB, TEV, Amplified, and is included only as a footnote in RSV and Phillips. Furthermore, this prediction is unrelated to the Holy Spirit. It is "them that believe" who "shall speak with new tongues." This prediction is, however, associated with some questionable practices such as the taking up of serpents and the drinking of "some deadly thing." If this scripture binds believers to one practice it binds them to all. And there are some "snake handling" fanatics who believe that, and practice it.

If "tongues" are of such importance, why do the gospels not give *examples*, and some sound information and guidance regarding their use? Or by any chance does Jesus indeed give further guidance when He admonished: "When you pray, do not keep on babbling like pagans, for they think they will be heard because of their many words" (Matt. 6:7, NIV)?

If "tongues" are so important for all believers, why does Paul give guidance only to the church at Corinth? and James, John, and Peter to none at all?

If "tongues" are so important, why do the accounts of the vibrant Early Church in Jerusalem given in Acts 2:41-47 and 4:31-37, obviously of Spirit-filled believers, make no mention whatever of their "speaking in tongues?" And why this omission regarding *every other* church mentioned in Acts and in the Epistles? There is a total blank on tongue-speaking in any church but Corinth.

"Tongues" as a gift of the Spirit is mentioned in Acts 2, 10, and 19; and in one Epistle, 1 Corinthians, chapters 12 and 14. That is all!

2. The Nature of Tongues in the Scriptures

Etymologically, "tongues"—in the Old Testament Hebrew (lashon) and in the New Testament Greek (glōssa)—means one of two things: either the organ of speech in the mouth (Judg. 7:5; Luke 16:24) or a national language (Gen. 10:5, "every one after his tongue, after their families, in their nations"; Rev. 5:9, "They sung a new song, saying, Thou art worthy to take the book, and to open the seals thereof: for thou wast slain, and hast redeemed us to God by thy blood out of every kindred, and tongue, and people, and nation"). For the complete use as "language" see also Rev. 7:9; 9:11; 10:11; 11:9; 13:7; 14:6; 16:16; 17:15. Modern translations use the word "language," both in the Old and the New Testament rather than "tongues" which was the term used when the King James Version was translated in 1611. The only present carryover is our use of the phrase "mother tongue."

On the Day of Pentecost the record in Acts 2 indicates clearly that they spoke in various languages as the Spirit gave them utterance. For the Scripture says of the listening multitude: "They were confounded, because that every man heard them speak in his own language. And they were amazed." These men speaking were all Galileans and would not necessarily know these foreign languages. "How hear we every man in our own tongue, wherein we were born?" And there follows a listing of some 14 countries. Since Acts was written after Paul wrote First Corinthians, was Luke purposely emphasizing the nationality of the languages used on the Day of Pentecost?

It is puzzling to note that a nationally known charismatic leader has declared, "In *each* recorded incident of a baptism of the Holy Spirit in Acts, speaking in a *heavenly* language or *unknown tongue* was emphasized."

The tongues may have been unknown to the disciples, but not to the people from the several nations who listened. And how do those tongues become "heavenly language?" It is from irresponsible statements like this that mistaken concepts arise concerning the supposed significance of "tongues" in the Early Church and in today's church.

There are some who say that at Pentecost the miracle was in the hearing. This appears less than likely, however, in that the Scripture distinctly designates the working of the Spirit to be, not on the ungodly crowd, "as the Spirit gave them understanding," but on the speakers, the disciples, "as the Spirit gave them utterance."

There are two and only two other recorded accounts in the Book of Acts of people speaking with "tongues," one in chapter 11 and the other in chapter 19. The first tells of Cornelius and the other of the 12 disciples in Ephesus. In view of the fact that all three accounts were recorded by the same writer, Luke, there is no reason to think that there was in his mind a change of meaning of the word *glōssa*. No translation was needed in any of the instances, a fact accepted by a broad representation of commentators such as Adam Clarke; Matthew Henry; Jamieson, Fausset, and Brown; as well as more recent scholars, such as Duewel, Carter, Gromacki, Taylor, Gustafson, Oke, Purkiser. They spoke in *established foreign languages* at Pentecost and also on these two other occasions.

The total use of *glōssa* in the New Testament as referring to speech is limited to four books: Mark (16:17), Acts

(2:4-11; 10:46; 19:6), 1 Corinthians (chapters 12 and 14), and Revelation as noted above.

KJV is inconsistent in that the italicized term "unknown" tongues is introduced in 1 Cor. 14:2. Nor is this "manufactured" term used consistently in that chapter, nor is it used elsewhere. "Tongues" is the term used throughout KJV for *glōssa*. For some reason, NASB uses "tongues" throughout, even in the Book of Revelation, though there seems no justification for it.

NEB is erratic in its choice of expressions. While properly using "language" in the Book of Revelation, it gives the translation "tongues" in Acts 2:4 and 11, then changes without any apparent linguistic authority, to "ecstatic utterance," "gift of ecstatic utterance," "tongue of ecstasy," and "language of ecstasy" in Acts 10:46; 19:6; and in 1 Corinthians chapters 12 and 14. On the subject of "tongues," this version offers no clarification.

NIV is the most consistent and helpful, in that it presents in footnotes an alternate expression of "or language," or "or other languages" throughout both the books of Acts and 1 Corinthians. Also, it consistently uses the word "languages" in the book of Revelation.

Concerning the "tongues" used by Cornelius (Acts 10:46), Peter was saying that this gift to Cornelius also was in a viable language, unlearned by the speakers, but known to the listeners. This was underscored when he commented that the Holy Spirit fell on Cornelius *"as on us at the beginning"* (Acts 11:15-17), and that God gave them the like gift *"as he did unto us,"* referring, of course, to the Upper Room experience.

When this phenomenon occurred at Ephesus, Luke states that "they began speaking with tongues and prophesied" (Acts 19:6). Both Adam Clarke and Matthew Henry take the position that this "prophesying" was preaching in the miraculously given "tongues" *(glōssais)* to a people who could not have comprehended the gospel message distinctly without that assistance. This conclusion appears quite justified.

There are two further aspects of the use of "tongues" as recorded in Acts. First, no translation was needed and none was used; indeed, no "gift of translation" was given. The national languages served their purpose to the persons who understood them. And, secondly, there *was* a purpose in their use at that time and in that place.

Another fact of importance is that there is no record in the Book of Acts of the repeated or continued use of the gift of languages—either in Jerusalem, or in Caesarea, or in Ephesus. The gift of healing was predominant in the Early Church, together with miracles, the casting out of demons, the gifts of prophecy and of teaching. Certainly there were manifest such gifts as evangelism, encouragement, ministry, showing mercy, and of helps throughout the New Testament. But no repetition is recorded in the Book of Acts or mention of any continued use of the gift of languages, and never that of interpretation. Surely it is a false picture presented by the charismatics that the Early Church everywhere was a church of "tongue speaking" members! This has to be merely a figment of the imagination, rather than the record in the Word.

Charles Carter makes a strong case that there were in Corinth perversions of the genuine gift of languages.

> The tongues problem at Corinth obviously consisted in a confusion and consequent counterfeiting of the genuine, miraculously bestowed gift of bona fide languages, such as was experienced at the Jerusalem Pentecost, at Caesarea, and at Ephesus. Some Corinthian Christians apparently introduced into the church elements of the unintelligible ecstatic utterances used by the worshippers of Aphrodite and Cybele at Corinth, and elsewhere in the ancient world . . .
>
> Some in the church at Corinth may have heard

about, or even observed, the bona fide gift of languages, and then confused that phenomenon with the ecstatic "unknown utterances" at the pagan shrines. Having been addicted to the latter, they carried these pagan practices into the church, where they sought to display their misdirected talents in competition with those who spoke with the genuine gift of languages to witness to people of foreign speech who were present in their services. . . . Thus subjunctive, if not sometimes demoniacal, ecstatic experiences with which Paul dealt in his Corinthian correspondence were either intentional or ignorant counterfeits of the genuine, divinely given experiences of bona fide languages (see 1 Cor. 12:1-3).[1]

3. The Purpose of Tongues in the Early Church

No one will propose that tongues were scattered carelessly from the hand of God. He must have had a divine purpose.

a. If foreign or national languages are accepted as the gift in the three instances in Acts, the purpose there seems to be twofold—evangelism, and the validation of the new covenant relationship.

Evangelism certainly was accomplished on the Day of Pentecost. The gospel regarding "the wonderful works of God" was transmitted in their own languages to people of many countries and dialects. And that convincingly, in view of the 3,000 souls who "received his word, were baptized: and . . . were added unto them" (Acts 2:41).

Cornelius had a large "household" of some 300-600 Roman guards from all over the world, representing many languages. Is it not fair to suppose that, hearing God magnified by those of Cornelius' household in their own languages, these men were moved and they too became messengers among their own people? This would also seem to be corroborated by Peter's statement "as on us at the beginning," when indeed the gospel was preached.

Ephesus was a wicked, polyglot, multiracial city, the center of gross immorality in connection with idolatry. Shortly after the descent of the Spirit and the outbreak of languages, a revival descended, a fortune in books of the occult was burned, a riot ensued—and a church was born, a church of no small dimensions.

Evangelism—a witness in Jerusalem, Samaria, and the uttermost part of the earth—was accomplished in the power of the Spirit.

It is interesting to note again that in neither of these cities was interpretation needed. These were bona fide gifts of viable languages conferred by the Spirit. And that "language of the Spirit" was understood by those who heard it.

In each of these instances, the giving of language skills appears also to have been used by God to validate the new covenant relationship—with the Jews of Jerusalem in Acts 2; with the Romans in Caesarea in Acts 10; and with the heathen of Ephesus in Acts 19. This validation can be compared to the superscription on the cross "in letters of Greek, and Latin, and Hebrew," that all might read: "THIS IS THE KING OF THE JEWS" (Luke 23:38).

b. In the case of the church at Corinth the purpose and accomplishment of tongues are not so clear. If the believers were speaking in the church in established languages which they themselves had never learned, they were misusing a genuine gift of languages, which *may* have previously occurred at Corinth to aid in evangelism in that area but which now was not needed within the church, either for evangelism or for validating a covenant. Indeed, a translator was now needed to make sense. It was a vain display of an exciting, but impractical gift. It failed to build up the Church. It was divisive. People of the congregation did not understand it, only God did (14:2). You are building up yourself, not the church (vv. 3-4), said

Paul. Prophecy is much more productive. All real languages have a meaning. But unless you understand them, the speaker is a foreigner to you (vv. 6-11), and the speaking meaningless.

I have mastery of many languages in my position as a travelling evangelist, Paul said, but 10,000 words in a language you do not understand would be of much less benefit than 5 or 6 words you do understand (vv. 18-19). Don't be childish, he warned. Languages were given on the Day of Pentecost, and on the subsequent occasions, for sound purposes. You show your immaturity when you try to perpetuate the gift of language without any purpose (v. 20). And, if you must speak in those languages, you or someone else *must translate* (v. 27). And don't overdo it. Not more than two or three to a service. If there is no translator, then be quiet (v. 28).

Further, if they were speaking in ecstatic utterances they were not following the Pentecostal pattern in which there were living, meaningful languages used. So Paul was outlining sharp controls to keep them in line.

Note that "tongues" constitutes the one gift that had to be controlled, directed, and disciplined. Also it was a problem only to the Corinthian church, possibly because it was an assumed gift by an unspiritual people. There is no evidence that this gift was given them on the descent of the Holy Spirit. Indeed, the evidence is to the contrary. They were unspiritual people.

Far from being a guide encouraging the use of tongues, the 14th chapter of 1 Corinthians is intended as a correction of a tongue-speaking people. *Tongues, with them, were not fulfilling the purpose evident in the other instances recounted in the Book of Acts.*

4. Tongues and the Holy Spirit

In people's minds, tongues are properly or improperly

related to the Holy Spirit. The Scripture record on this is important.

First of all, tongues were neither predicted or promised, either as a *gift* of the Holy Spirit, or as a *fruit* of the Spirit, or as a *ministry* of the Spirit. To accompany an outpouring of the Spirit the promise was power (Acts 1:8). The evidence of the presence of the Spirit is fruit (Gal. 5:22).

It is to be noted, furthermore, that "tongues" did not ordinarily accompany the effusion of the Spirit. There were but the three occasions, already noted—in Jerusalem to the Jews (Acts 2:4); in Caesarea to Cornelius and his household (Acts 10:44-46), and in Ephesus to the 12 believers (Acts 19:6).

But there were numerous other occasions when the Spirit came *without* the gift of tongues: to Peter (Acts 4:8), to the assembled believers (4:31), to the Samaritans (8:15-17), to Saul of Tarsus (9:6, 17-18), to Paul (13:9), and to disciples (13:52). There is no record of speaking in tongues by such Spirit-filled men as the seven deacons chosen for special work (6:3-5), by Stephen (7:55), or by Barnabas (11:22-24). It is again to be recognized that the "gifted" Corinthian church, which did speak in some kind of tongues, was not a Spirit-filled church (1 Cor. 3:1), and therefore gives us no example of relationships between the baptism with the Holy Spirit and tongue-speaking.

The fact remains that there are no scriptural grounds, either in promise or example, to expect that there should be a gift of tongues accompanying an enduement with the Holy Spirit. The real purpose of the gift of the Holy Spirit is to cleanse hearts, to empower for righteous living, and to communicate the gospel. The pattern that is normal is found in Acts 4:31 where, after they were filled with the Holy Spirit, the believers began to speak, not with tongues, but "with boldness" in the gift of prophecy.

Furthermore, in reporting later what had happened to Cornelius' household it is most interesting to note, Peter said nothing about the gift of tongues. That did not impress him nearly as much as did the cleansing of their hearts (Acts 15:7-9). Could tongues be more purposefully omitted from the reports than by Peter on this occasion? Was it because they were inconsequential? only temporary? unavailable to others? One cannot be dogmatic.

But this is exactly what God's people must emphasize—not tongues but cleansing, not charisma but sanctification, not gifts but evangelism.

Jesus does give warning that "gifts" can be spurious. He warned:

> Not every one that saith unto me, Lord, Lord, shall enter into the kingdom of heaven; but he that doeth the will of my Father which is in heaven. Many will say to me in that day, Lord, Lord, have we not prophesied in thy name? and in thy name have cast out devils? and in thy name done many wonderful works? And then will I profess unto them, I never knew you: depart from me, ye that work iniquity (Matt. 7:21-23).

Satan can counterfeit gifts. Fruit he cannot. Ministries he cannot.

5. Tongues Today

A certain artificiality attends the practice of tongues-speaking today. In many instances a conscious effort is made to "generate" tongues. First of all, there must be a high pitch of excitement and expectancy and urgent request. But note that in all three instances listed in Acts, tongues were not received in response to a request. On the Day of Pentecost the gathered 120 had had no advance intimation whatever of such a "sign." Jesus, himself, had not received a gift of tongues when anointed with the Spirit, nor had He given the slightest hint of a prospect of such when He promised His disciples, "John truly baptized with water: but ye shall be baptized with the Holy Ghost not many days hence. . . . Ye shall receive power, after that the Holy Ghost is come upon you" (Acts 1:5, 8). There is not a suggestion in Peter's message to Cornelius that a "gift of tongues" awaited them. And the disciples at Ephesus were simply asked "Have ye received the Holy Ghost since ye believed?" There was no inquiry, intimation, nor promise regarding speaking in tongues.

Yet, today, certain exercises are often resorted to to get people to speak in tongues. Wayne A. Robinson tells of a candidate for tongues who was to repeat the following words with ever increasing rapidity, "Blessed Jesus, suffering Saviour, save the sin-sick souls of sinful sinners. We wait, willingly, wantingly, wonderfully, wistfully right now!" Fast, then slow; then fast again. When she began to mix up the words, he sped up the pace. Soon she was standing with her arms lifted high and tears streaming down her face while she repeated strange sounds. To the watching group, the pastor announced that she had received the infilling of the Spirit. What they were hearing, he said, was talking in tongues.[2]

Participants in seminars and classes I have conducted in many parts of the world have told of similar experiences, sometimes of their own participation. They have borne a similar character. Recently there was a very similar display on television where, at a large gathering the uninitiated were urged to follow a similar pattern of words: "God is great. God is good. God is glorious. Hallelujah, praise the Lord." Possessors of the gift were encouraged to help and demonstrate to the uninitiated sitting next to them. "Let your jaw hang loose" were the instructions by the leader. "Now manipulate it right, then left as you emit unenunciated sounds." By demonstration and assistance this was accomplished from one to another,

73

with an ever-increasing crescendo of sound, until that huge auditorium became bedlam, with chanting, shouting, ecstatic meaningless phrases, the waving of hands. The "Spirit" had come!

What is the language today of the tongues movement? There are those who contend that known, spoken languages of the world are being said. Snatches of German, Chinese, Italian supposedly are identified from time to time, spoken by one totally unfamiliar with the language. But any extended communication in a known language is hard to identify.

John Sherrill, who speaks for the charismatics, in an effort to prove the linguistic nature of tongues, brought together David Scott, religious book editor of McGraw-Hill, and six linguists in a private gathering. Among these men were two specialists in modern languages, three in ancient languages, and one an expert in language structure.

At this meeting Sherrill played several tapes which he had made of people speaking in tongues, and requested that the linguists try to see if they could identify any of these tongues as being a genuine language. Sherrill himself records the results.

> As I put on the first tape, each man leaned forward, straining to catch every syllable. Several took notes. But at no time did I see a face light up with recognition. I played another tape, and then another. For the better part of an hour we listened to one prayer after another, spoken "in the Spirit." And when, at last, we came to the end, I looked around and asked, "Well, gentlemen?" Six heads shook in the negative. *Not one had heard a language which he could identify.*[3]

Charismatics claim to "speak with other tongues as the Spirit gives them utterance *according to Acts 2:4.*" This is an oft repeated phrase. But they are hard put to prove it. God is simply not giving the skill to speak "according to

Acts 2:4." For that means using known, living, working languages of the world. Is it then the language of the Corinthians, presuming that *they* spoke in ecstatic utterances? That depends on one's interpretation of that Scripture, and on the purpose of present day glossolalia.

The personal experience of the writer should not be out of order here. I do witness to the fulness of the Spirit in my life, having received the Holy Spirit many years ago (over half a century), and presently enjoying the continued blessing of holiness. And I pray consistently the petition admonished by Jesus in Luke 11:13. In recent years my wife and I have been called to special service in conducting holiness institutes with national officers in Zaire, Rhodesia, Kenya, South Africa, Mexico, Korea, and Japan. In every case I personally made it a matter of earnest prayer that God might grant the facility to speak in the national language of the country without interpretation. God did not answer my prayers. Instead He provided excellent translators.

Indeed, God is just not thus bestowing upon missionaries, evangelists, and teachers the language of the country to which they are going! For reasons best known to himself, God has withdrawn the gift of languages which He extended in those three instances to the Early Church.

6/

THE EMPHASES OF THE
CHARISMATIC MOVEMENT

Someone has observed that, today, the Charismatic Renewal is essentially a prayer movement. And this cannot be all bad. One of the pressing needs today of the church as a whole is a deeper involvement in effectual, fervent prayer. If the charismatics set us a pattern in this, let us say, "Well done. May we profit by your example." Yet there is a facet of charismatic prayer that is disturbing—the labeling of "tongues" as a "prayer language."

1. The Prayer Language Issue

All the great prayers in the Bible were clearly spoken and recorded in a known language. Neither "tongues" nor "other languages" are even mentioned in the prayer life of David, Ezekiel, Isaiah—upon all of whom the Spirit came in power. Nor do we find it in the prayers of Jesus, of John, of Elizabeth and Mary, of Zacharias and Anna—all of whom were "filled with the Holy Spirit." The mighty, moving prayers of Paul are all recorded in the language of the day. Then through the centuries great men of the church, filled with the Holy Spirit, men of impressive prayer life, have not been known for ecstatic utterances, but for simple prayer petitions. Must the pattern change now?

Why did Jesus not give directions toward a prayer language when one of His disciples said to Him, "Lord, teach us to pray" (Luke 11:1)? Why, as with each of the other gifts mentioned in Corinthians, is the so-called "prayer language" available only to certain chosen persons? "All do not speak with tongues, do they?" (1 Cor. 12:30, NASB). And why are tongues listed last in the recounting of gifts in the order of their importance (1 Cor. 12:28-30)? And why were the Gentiles not directed to such a "prayer language" when the church conference, recorded in Acts 15, set up the list of "necessary things" for them?

These omissions are significant.

There are scriptures which the charismatic presents to support the practice of praying in tongues. In analyzing those from Paul, however, it must be remembered that, whenever he spoke of "tongues," he was striving to correct rather than to promote its use.

There is the statement in 1 Cor. 13:1: "Though I speak with the tongues of men and of angels, and have not charity, I am become as sounding brass, or a tinkling cymbal." Paul had been saying two things. There is an order of importance among the gifts, of which "tongues" are in last place, and the believer is to "covet earnestly the best gifts." Secondly he has continued by declaring that there is "a more excellent way" than that of gifts—any and all gifts. That is the way of *love*. O Corinthians, who lay such a stress on gifts and particularly on tongues, there is a more excellent way!

Then consider "the tongues of angels." There is no evidence that angels have a special "tongue." When they appeared they spoke to men in the languages known to men, with no need of translation. This was true whether it was in Old Testament days—to Hagar (Gen. 16:8), to Jacob (Gen. 31:11), to Gideon (Judg. 6:20);—or the New Testament days—to Zacharias (Luke 1:11), to Mary (Luke 1:26), to the shepherds (Luke 2:9). In his letter to the Corinthians, Paul was not speaking of any special language of men or of angels, but of the fluency, the eloquence of one or the other. If exercised without love—as was true with the Corinthians—such eloquence is only noisy and empty.

Paul continues in chapter 14 to discuss that which is often taken to mean prayer language. "Pursue love, yet desire earnestly spiritual gifts, but especially that you may prophesy. For one who speaks in a tongue does not speak to men, but to God; for no one understands, but in his spirit he speaks mysteries. But one who prophesies speaks to men for edification and exhortation and consolation" (1 Cor. 14:1-3, NASB). He then continues, "One who speaks in a tongue edifies himself; but one who prophesies edifies the church. Now I wish that you all spoke in tongues, but even more that you would prophesy; and greater is one who prophesies than one who speaks in tongues, unless he interprets, so that the church may receive edifying" (vv. 4-5).

Obviously Paul is here struggling with a practice which was not altogether desirable. "Tongues" were taking the place of prophecy but, more importantly, of love.

The purpose of gifts was not edification of self, but of "the church"—"for the common good" (1 Cor. 12:7, NASB). Unless languages are interpreted (even in talking to God) they do not serve the purpose of evangelism and mutual edification for which gifts are given. And, beyond that, the fruit of the Spirit is to be "eagerly desired" above any of the gifts.

Specifically, Paul was *willing (thelo,* acquiescence) that all should speak in languages (v. 5), but much more desirous that they spoke so that they might be understood by all, whether by means of that national language which was used by the people or, at least, by translation.

Later in chapter 14 Paul speaks directly to the matter of praying "in a tongue." But let it be noted here that the very heart of chapter 14 is a clear-cut plea regarding the necessity of *meaningful communication.* In vv. 7-12 Paul declares:

> Even in the case of lifeless things that make sounds, such as the flute or harp, how will anyone know what tune is being played unless there is a sharp distinction in the notes? Again, if the trumpet does not sound a clear call, who will get ready for battle? So it is with you. Unless you speak intelligible words with your tongue, how will anyone know what you are saying? You will just be speaking into the air. Undoubtedly there are all sorts of languages in the world, yet none of them is without meaning. If then I do not grasp the meaning of what someone is saying, I am a foreigner to the speaker, and he is a foreigner to me. So it is with you. Since you are eager to have spiritual gifts, try to excel in gifts that build up the church (NIV).

Verses 14-16 are much used by the charismatic to support praying in ecstatic tongues by the Holy Spirit without the assistance of the mind. But let a second principle governing chapter 14 here be noted. There is *no solid evidence* of the Holy Spirit being in the chapter at all!

Clearly He is identified in chapter 12, as "the Spirit of God," "the Holy Ghost" (v. 3), "the same Spirit" (vv. 4, 8, 9), "the selfsame Spirit" (v. 11), the "one Spirit" (v. 13). He is properly identified throughout that chapter with a capital S.

However, the spirit of chapter 14 is identified as "my spirit" (v. 14), the believer's own spirit. Although in the other verses there are alternate margin references in some translations to Spirit with a capital S, yet the first translation of all versions throughout chapter 14 is identified by a small s (vv. 2, 14, 15, 16). Any doctrine of speaking, or singing in "tongues" by the influence of the Holy Spirit has very doubtful support from 1 Corinthians, chapter 14, from which apparently the Holy Spirit had fled.

In the light of these two governing principles for the chapter, note that Paul now addresses himself to praying "in an unknown tongue," that is, in *a language not understood by the hearers,* whatever language that may be. "If I pray in an unknown tongue," he says, "my spirit prayeth, but my understanding is unfruitful," that is, it bears no fruit, carries no comprehension to the listener. Wuest translates this, "My intellect confers no benefit upon others." Williams expresses it, "My mind produces no results for anyone." While the Amplified adds, "My mind bears no fruit and helps nobody." It is a case of failing to have *meaningful communication.* "What is it then?" continues Paul. "I will pray with the spirit, and I will pray with the understanding also; I will sing with the spirit, and I will sing with the understanding also. Else when thou shalt bless with the spirit, how shall he that occupieth the room of the unlearned say Amen at thy giving of thanks, seeing he understandeth not what thou sayest?" *The understanding that counts is on the part of the hearer.*

The language I use in witnessing, in praying, and in

singing must make a *comprehensible communication* if it is to benefit anybody. Therefore, I will speak, pray, sing *to be understood,* so that the "unlearned" may say "amen" at the right time, so that all may be edified and God be glorified!

The message of this chapter remains a plea for *comprehensible communication,* and leaves as *very dubious* any participation by the Holy Spirit in speaking, praying, or singing in "unknown tongues."

Then there is Rom. 8:26. Here the scripture is clearly referring to the aid of the Holy Spirit to the believer in his prayer life. It is a most important verse.

Paul has been speaking in that chapter about deliverance by the Spirit (v. 2), "walking after the Spirit" (vv. 4 ff.), a bodily resurrection "by His Spirit" (v. 11); being "led by the Spirit" (v. 14), receiving "the Spirit of adoption" (vv. 15-17). He now climaxes this summary of the work of the Spirit with the stirring statement, "In the same way the Spirit also helps our weakness; for we do not know how to pray as we should, but the Spirit Himself intercedes for us with groanings too deep for words; and He who searches the hearts knows what the mind of the Spirit is, because He intercedes for the saints according to the will of God" (Rom. 8:26-27, NASB).

The verb "helps" is a most interesting, meaningful, multisyllable word in the Greek, expressed here in the middle voice. Vine points out that it "signifies to take hold with at the side for assistance; hence, to take a share in, help in bearing, help in general."[1] Of the middle voice Mantey says, "English knows no approximate parallel . . . but the middle voice is that use of the verb which describes the subject as *participating in the results of the action.*"[2] Thus we have a strong expression of the co-operative help of the Holy Spirit in the burden of our prayer life. Unhappy is the person who has never been so burdened—and so assisted.

The verb is used in only one other place in the New Testament—Luke 10:40. It is contained in Martha's request to the Lord to bid her sister help her in preparing dinner. There it is in the urgent aorist tense of "right now." "Lord, dost thou not care that my sister hath left me to serve [thee] alone? bid her therefore that she [take hold on the other side—right now—and] help me."

But the verb is also used in the Septuagint of Num. 11:17. Moses has complained, "I alone am not able to carry all this people, because it is too burdensome for me" (v. 14, NASB). Consequently God tells him to gather 70 men of the elders of the people that they might stand with him. God then declares, "Then I will come down and speak with you there, and I will take of the Spirit who is upon you, and will put Him upon them; and they *shall bear the burden* of the people *with you,* so that you shall not bear it all alone" (italics added).

Thus, as the Paraclete, the Holy Spirit *can be called alongside* where He will "lend a hand with us on the other side" in our prayer life, where He will "bear the burden with us." The "weakness" which Paul speaks of may be that we lack guidance regarding the *subject* for prayer—the "what" of KJV, NIV; or regarding the *manner* of our prayer—the "how" of NASB, NEB. The Greek will accommodate either. But what a promise to a believer in the agonizing burden of prayer! The *New English Bible* puts it meaningfully:

> In the same way the Spirit comes to the aid of our weakness. We do not even know how we ought to pray [or what it is right to pray for, marg.], but through our inarticulate groans the Spirit himself is pleading for us, and God who searches our inmost being knows what the Spirit means, because he pleads for God's own people in God's own way.

This, says the charismatic, constitutes the "heavenly language" of prayer. To others it simply means that our entirely inadequate language, our limited vocabulary, our halting delivery, likened to groanings "too deep for words," is translated by Him into intercession understood by God, which will not be denied us. Note that they are "sighs," "groans," not words, quite apparently not a "language" as such, for a spoken "language" must have words. They are expressions any child of God will manifest under great burden and concern. As Duewel expresses it: "This is not a description of man praying with the gift of tongues; this is a description of God the Holy Spirit praying with such deep yearning that it goes beyond all language."[3]—Is it not a description of how God the Son, our other *Paraclete*, prays for us at the throne of God—with deep yearning that goes beyond all language? (See 1 John 2:12; Heb. 7:25.)

James Montgomery has caught something of this in his hymn:

> *Prayer is the soul's sincere desire*
> *Uttered or unexpressed,*
> *The motion of a hidden fire*
> *That trembles in the breast.*

> *Prayer is the burden of a sigh,*
> *The falling of a tear,*
> *The upward glancing of an eye*
> *When none but God is near.*

In summary, certain principles are clear, concerning the matter of "prayer language."

a. "Prayer language" is neither *a* sign or *the* sign of the baptism with the Holy Spirit. It isn't so promised, nor was it so provided according to Scripture. If it should be considered to be a gift, it is given only by the sovereign will of God, not by the will or request of man. And all cannot receive it. Again, such a "prayer language" shall not be used in public, except there be an interpretation.

Further, Paul declared that if anyone is to desire a gift he should earnestly covet the "best" gifts, and the gift of "tongues" is not among "the best gifts," so why seek it?

b. It must be recognized that this is not the gift of a "Pentecostal" language as of Acts 2. For on that day the languages were discernible, understandable, currently used, and given for the propagation of the faith to others.

c. It is questionable how such an implied "prayer language" could fulfill the purpose of gifts, in that Paul declared that gifts are manifest "for the common good," "for the equipping of the saints for the work of service," and Peter proclaimed, "As each one has received a special gift, employ it in serving one another."

d. Finally, it is questionable whether "prayer language" today is actually a scriptural gift from the Holy Spirit. It has been established that it is not a practice to be associated with the outpouring of the Spirit; that it is not the language of Pentecost or of the Early Church as recorded in Acts; that it fails to fulfill the declared purpose of the valid gifts of the Spirit; that it was not used by Jesus himself, or by the prayer warriors of the centuries; that there is no valid scriptural evidence that such a "prayer language" was used by any of the apostles, or by the Apostolic Church (unless in certain mistaken instances by the unspiritual church in Corinth), and that it is not associated in 1 Corinthians 14 with the Holy Spirit.

Then, if not scriptural, and if not historical, can this "prayer language" in actual fact be more than a subjective experience—psychological, emotional, irrational—which is not divinely given nor sponsored nor encouraged?

Great prayers are those voiced in a language which is understood by the hearers as well as by the one who prays. Of course God understands all languages.

2. The Charismatic Movement and the Scriptures

In a Christian gathering recently the question arose, "But speaking in tongues *is* scriptural, isn't it?" The reference was to today's practice of ecstatic utterance. This is a question which invites investigation.

As far as speaking in tongues through the motivation of the Holy Spirit is concerned, there are two areas of Scripture involved—the Book of Acts and First Corinthians. It isn't mentioned elsewhere.

The Book of Acts, of course, is the historic record of the Early Church. Here the obvious answer is no. Speaking in tongues today is not according to the pattern of the Early Church. There are several reasons for the negative answer.

As was noted earlier, the gift of "tongues" was manifest in the Scripture in connection with the enduement of the Holy Spirit in only three instances, Acts 2, 10, and 19. Several other occasions are recorded where the gift of the Spirit was received but where there was no such gift of languages.

It has been noted that in the three instances the gift was a gift of *known* and currently used *languages.* This is particularly identified in Acts 2:4-11. But Peter twice identified, in Acts 11:17 and Acts 15:8, that the gift of the Holy Spirit to Cornelius' household, recorded in Acts 10:44-46, was "a like gift" to that of the day of Pentecost. Furthermore, note that in none of the three instances in Acts was interpretation necessary for the understanding of the evangelistic message which was proclaimed.

In addition, rules of translation of the Scripture require that, unless otherwise stated, the same word within one book by one writer be given the same meaning—in this case "language" for *glōssa.*

Today's practice of tongue-speaking is not that of the

Early Church as recorded in Acts. For God today is not giving the ability to speak in foreign languages, even to those who would profit by such a gift, such as missionaries. Why? That is His decision, just as it was His decision not to give such a gift to all believers at that time.

The Book of First Corinthians is considered separately. If it be accepted that *glōssa* here also means known and used languages, as attested to by the majority of writers and commentators, then the case is not different, and speaking in ecstatic tongues is not scriptural. If, however, it is granted that the Corinthians spoke in ecstatic utterances, the case needs careful examination.

First of all, the experience would be theirs alone. There is no inference that any other church—at Jerusalem, Ephesus, Galatia, or elsewhere—spoke in ecstatic tongues. And, to the Corinthians, particular corrective guidance was given.

Tongues constituted the least important gift, and much less important than love, the fruit of the Spirit. It was not available to all (12:29-30), was unprofitable in public meetings (14:19), and was a childish practice (14:20). It was to be sharply limited to two or three participants, and must be followed by interpretation (14:27-28). It was not evangelistic and church building, but self-serving (14:2-4).

Particularly remember the two principles which apply to 1 Corinthians 14. The heart of the chapter (vv. 7-12) is a plea for *comprehensible communication*. And there is no clear evidence of the Holy Spirit being in the chapter at all, rather it is the spirit of the believer in verse 14, which governs the use of a small s for spirit throughout the chapter. It is "my spirit."

If the speaking in tongues today is the same ecstatic utterances presumably exhibited by the Corinthians, several unhappy and unsavory facts need to be remembered. That church was a schismatic congregation, contentious, unspiritual, carnal, childish, harboring envy, strife, and divisions (1:1-13; 3:1-5). Even more serious shortcomings were the gross immorality of some and the callous indifference of others (5:1-13), the lawsuits brought one against another within the church (6:1-8), questionable marital practices (7:1-5), their compromising attitude toward idolatry (8:1-13).

Is speaking in tongues scriptural? Only if one accepts the weakness of a carnal, first-century church to be a "scriptural" record. But one could hardly accept it as spiritually directed or endorsed.

As we admire the earnest evangelical efforts of the charismatics, and join in rejoicing over souls won, there can well be puzzled questions in our minds regarding their apparently unscriptural zeal for the spectacular gifts, and particularly for that questionable gift of ecstatic tongues.

3. Divine Healing

Divine healing is also proclaimed and emphasized by the charismatics. "Miracle services" are held. Prayer for the sick is featured, laying on of hands practiced, healings witnessed to and demonstrated. Undoubtedly many healings are accomplished, though some of it doubtless is psychosomatic in nature.

Indeed all ardent Christians believe in divine healing. All healing is the work of God, whether done by prayer and faith, or by the skilled surgeon's scalpel, or by suitable diet, exercise, medicine, and drugs.

God does perform miracles of healing today. As a boy I saw this happen in our own household when my mother was miraculously healed of recurring and persistent illnesses. And what child of God has not seen God's hand in the healing of a loved one or himself, and who does not give Him the glory for a healthy body and reasonable daily health and strength! Yes, we believe in divine healing. *But not on demand.*

There are two areas where God's will is the same for every person—for all mankind. God "wills" that all should be saved. First Timothy 2:4 says of Him, "Who wants all men to be saved and to come to a knowledge of the truth" (NIV). Second Peter 3:9 proclaims in like fashion, "The Lord is not slack concerning his promise, as some men count slackness; but is longsuffering to us-ward, not willing that any should perish, but that all should come to repentance."

God also "wills" that every believer should be sanctified. First Thessalonians 4:1-8 says, in part:

> Furthermore then we beseech you, brethren, and exhort you by the Lord Jesus, that as ye have received of us how ye ought to walk and to please God, so ye would abound more and more. For ye know what commandments we gave you by the Lord Jesus. For this is the will of God, even your sanctification, that ye should abstain from fornication: that every one of you should know how to possess his vessel in sanctification and honour. . . . For God hath not called us unto uncleanness, but unto holiness. He therefore that despiseth, despiseth not man, but God, who hath also given unto us his holy Spirit.

The will of God regarding healing for everyone is not thus stated, even though texts are quoted to the contrary.

For example, Isa. 53:5 is strongly cited as making healing an inseparable part of the atonement—"With his stripes we are healed"—not will be, not may be, but *are* healed! Let it be noted, however, that this is proclaimed in the company of such words as "transgressions," "iniquities," "peace," "iniquity." "He was wounded for our transgressions, he was bruised for our iniquities: the chastisement of our peace was upon him; and with his stripes we are healed." Obviously the affliction, the wounding, the bruising of our Saviour is directed to spiritual redemption, to spiritual healing.

Furthermore, the Hebrew word *rafa* is more often used in the figurative sense of healing of spiritual sickness than of the healing of the physical diseases. Isaiah 6:10 for example says, "Make the heart of this people fat, and make their ears heavy, and shut their eyes; lest they see with their eyes, and hear with their ears, and understand with their heart, and convert, and be healed." In like fashion see also Ps. 41:4; 147:3; Isa. 19:22; 30:26; Jer. 6:14; 8:11; 33:6; Hosea 6:1; 11:3. Physical healing must take a second place to the spiritual.

Peter has a strong commentary on this verse in Isaiah. First Peter 2:24 clearly refers to the *spiritual* healing of "our sins . . . unto righteousness" as a result of Christ's suffering: "Who his own self bare our sins in his own body on the tree, that we, being dead to sins, should live unto righteousness; by whose stripes ye were healed." Then he continues the account of the "healing" ministry as a spiritual reconciliation with the statement, "Ye were as sheep going astray; but are now returned unto the Shepherd and Bishop of your souls" (v. 25).

Sometimes in response to requests for healing, God says no. This He did three times to Paul regarding his "thorn in the flesh" (2 Cor. 12:7-10). God taught Paul that God's strength is made perfect in such weakness, and that he should actually "glory" in, "take pleasure" in, such infirmities, that "the power of Christ" might rest upon him. Paul had gifts of healing (Acts 28:8-9), yet he left Trophimus, a cherished co-worker, sick at Miletus (2 Tim. 4:20). He urged Timothy to take care of a weak stomach with a home remedy (1 Tim. 5:23).

The Scripture does not say that God will have *all men*

to be healed, and to be in perfect health. History has recorded, and we have all known, many saints of God to whom God said No, but who served Him in a remarkable fashion in their physical infirmity.

Concerning Christ's comment in Mark 16:17, "These signs will accompany those who have believed . . . they will lay hands on the sick, and they will recover" (NASB), several things may be said. One is that the section of Scripture is less than reliable, from vv. 9 through 20. Another is that if this command is to be taken as literal, the portion of this scripture which speaks about protection against poisonous snakes and poison also must be taken literally.

Careful consideration must be given to the message of Jas. 5:14-16.

> Is any sick among you? let him call for the elders of the church; and let them pray over him, anointing him with oil in the name of the Lord: and the prayer of faith shall save the sick, and the Lord shall raise him up; and if he have committed sins, they shall be forgiven him. Confess your faults one to another, and pray one for another, that ye may be healed. The effectual fervent prayer of a righteous man availeth much.

Let it be clearly said that healings do occur, that there are Spirit-anointed people who do pray the prayer of faith for healing, and that prayers of the righteous do prevail. However, as the *Interpreter's Bible* comments on this passage, "Both he and his readers know perfectly well that not all cases of sickness will be healed; here as always when the efficacy of prayer is taught, the condition 'if it be God's will' is to be tacitly understood."[4]

A comparable promise by Jesus must be examined in a similar light: "All things, whatsoever ye shall ask in prayer, believing, ye shall receive" (Matt. 21:22). All things? Another statement by Jesus recorded in John 15:7 is enlightening: "If ye abide in me, and my words abide in you, ye shall ask what ye will, and it shall be done unto you." What ye will? If we abide in Him and His words abide in us, *our will will be God's will.* Is not Jesus declaring the importance of ascertaining God's will so that our requests may be within it? And does this not apply to the healing of the sick as promised in James? Therefore the statement in Jas. 5:14-16 should be paired with Jesus' statement in John 15:7 for the proper interpretation of the text in question. "In the name of the Lord" comes to mean, "If it is ascertained to be the will of the Lord."

Thus again, in the will of God only two things are the same for all people—their salvation and their sanctification. Otherwise, God's will varies for each individual, including his health and his healing.

It is to be noted that large portions of the Scripture report no miracles. Many men, mighty in the Lord, performed none. Actually, miracles are bunched together into four clusters—those of Moses, of Elijah and Elisha, of Jesus, and of the apostles. This does not make the other "heroes of the faith" any less notable, whether B.C. or A.D. Nothing derogatory is implied in saying that no miracles are recorded for Abel, for Enoch, for Noah, for Abraham, Isaac, Jacob, or Joseph. No lack of faith is attributed for lack of miracles wrought by Gideon, David, Samuel, and the other prophets. John the Baptist, of whom Jesus testified, "Verily I say unto you, among them that are born of women there hath not risen a greater than John the Baptist," is specifically said to have performed no miracles (John 10:41). Nor should the stalwarts of the church through the ages be assigned to any minor role because they were not given to miracle working. The fact remains that it is apparent that miracles were given to attest four main epochs of revelation, namely, the law, the prophets, the coming of the Messiah, and the establishment of the age of the Holy Spirit as accomplished through the apostles.

Physical healing is not an amendment added to the gospel. It is God's sincere plan and purpose to meet all our human needs, including our healing and health, but only *according to His will.*

4. Eschatology

As previously noted, a third important tenet of faith of the Charismatic Renewal is the *imminent return* of Jesus Christ. Great stress is laid upon this expectation. Prophecies are quoted to prove it. "Within 10 years," "Before the turn of the century," "Within our lifetime"— these are among the bold statements being released with much fervor and excitement.

While a wide range of scriptural prophecies and latter-day signs are quoted to establish this, the claim that the "latter rain" is upon us is basic to the proclamation. Joel declares (2:23, 28-32):

> Be glad then, ye children of Zion, and rejoice in the Lord your God: for he hath given you the former rain moderately, and he will cause to come down for you the rain, the former rain, and the latter rain in the first month . . .

> And it shall come to pass afterward, that I will pour out my spirit upon all flesh; and your sons and your daughters shall prophesy, and your old men shall dream dreams, your young men shall see visions: and also upon the servants and upon the handmaids in those days will I pour out my spirit. And I will shew wonders in the heavens and in the earth, blood, and fire, and pillars of smoke. The sun shall be turned into darkness, and the moon into blood, before the great and the terrible day of the Lord come. And it shall come to pass, that whosoever shall call on the name of the Lord shall be delivered.

This, of course, was quoted (without reference to the

rain, however) by Peter, recorded in Acts 2:17-21; and apparently alluded to by James in 5:7: "Be patient, therefore, brethren, unto the coming of the Lord. Behold, the husbandman waiteth for the precious fruit of the earth, and hath long patience for it, until he receive the early and latter rain."

The charismatic interpretation of this is that the Apostolic Church brought in the firstfruits under the "former rain," while the charismatic church is chosen and ordained of God to bring in the "latter rain" in the lastfruits of the great harvest, which immediately precedes the Second Advent.

Frank Bartleman, after reviewing the revivals of the church under Luther and Wesley, writes thus:

> Here we are with the restoration of the very experience of "Pentecost," with the "latter rain," a restoration of the power ... to finish up the work begun. We shall again be lifted to the church's former level, to complete her work, begin where they left off when failure overtook them, and speedily fulfilling the last great commission, open the way for the coming of Christ.[5]

Tongues, healings, miracles—these are signs of the latter rain according to the Neo-Pentecostals. "This is God's final great movement of power to provide a strong witness to the church and the world before the coming of the Lord Jesus Christ," declares another. Has this not been claimed before? At any rate, history will prove the accuracy or the error of these predictions.

5. An Appraisal of the Charismatic Movement

There are a number of apparent deficiencies in the Charismatic Movement.

a. It presents a doctrine based primarily on personal experience and on isolated passages of Scripture rather than on the general teaching and emphasis of the Word. It is to be remembered that *"all* scripture . . . is profitable for doctrine" (italics added). A text apart from its context can become a pretext. And experience can be conditioned, subjective, opinionated, even biased.

b. Physical phenomena should not be taken as the proof for spiritual maturity and God's approval. Indeed, the real evidence of being Spirit-filled is a spiritual cleansing as reported in Acts 15:7-9, and spiritual fruit as described in Gal. 5:22-23.

c. The Charismatic Movement emphasizes two gifts which the Scriptures say are not for all believers. Actually, many ministries of the Spirit are listed which indeed are available and needed by all. And, as has been pointed out, other gifts of the Spirit are given priority in the Bible.

d. While the announced purpose of the Spirit is to glorify Jesus, and to promote Christlikeness in the believer, it focuses attention on the Spirit even above Jesus. It is in the movement of the Spirit the charismatics find excitement and spiritual thrills.

e. It intimates that through the centuries the church has been lacking in an experience which, according to them, is the promise of the Father, and the central sign of Christianity.

f. It emphasizes the emotional aspect of relationship to God, rather than a balanced approach involving body, mind, and spirit.

g. Its priorities seem to be power, excitement, and the spectacular rather than the quiet, divine miracle of cleansing, purity, sanctification, and holy living. It has been admitted in my seminars by those who once spoke in tongues that an exciting session with "tongues" can act as a palliative to a guilty conscience, and take the place of an act of confession and repentance, a request for forgiveness, and the forsaking of sins committed. A trenchant

94

comment is made in *God, Man, and Salvation,* "When Christians become infected by a lust for religious excitement, simple goodness gradually begins to seem tame. The passion for holiness is displaced by a passion for religious fireworks. This quickly degenerates into pseudo-spirituality."[6]

6. In Summary

There are positive influences being exerted by godly men in this movement who are persuaded of their position and are sincere in their profession. Evangelicals are being prodded into a new awareness of the Holy Spirit, into a new searching as to what the Word really says about Him. Christians of every denomination are challenged to analyze carefully the movement, weigh it by the Word of God, recognize its excesses, dangers, and errors, but also utilize the momentum of its spiritual thrust. *For today IS the age of the Holy Spirit.*

It may also be well remembered that Paul spoke to all Spirit-filled Christians when he said, "The body is not one member, but many." And again, "There should be no schism in the body; but that the members should have the same care one for another."

When Commissioner Brengle landed in Scandinavia early in this century he was accosted by some brethren who said, "Have you received the Holy Spirit?" When the answer was affirmative, they pressed the issue, "But we mean, have you spoken in tongues? Do you have the evidence?" When Brengle answered that he had not, they declared, "Then you do not have the blessing."

Very humbly and quietly the visiting Salvationist said, "Brethren, if there is anything further for me which God wants me to have, I'm open. Pray for me. In the meanwhile, come to the meetings."

Then he preached night after night on sanctification and perfect love—and, lo, these very men were among the first to come to *his* altar, seeking the experience of a purified heart.

7/

THE GIFT OR THE BAPTISM
OF THE HOLY SPIRIT

Under the Old Covenant, the Holy Spirit was bestowed by God's sovereign choice on selected people only, and usually that they might perform special tasks. For example, the Spirit of God came upon a Balaam that he might speak a parable (Num. 24:2); upon a Bezaleel that he might have wisdom, understanding, and skills to build furniture for the Tabernacle and the ark of testimony and the altar of incense (Exod. 31:3); upon a Gideon that he might deliver the nation (Judg. 6:34); upon a lad called David that he might rule the nation (1 Sam. 16:13); upon men like Ezekiel to be prophets (Ezek. 3:24); and upon those who would record God's message for mankind—the Scriptures (2 Pet. 1:21).

Since the New Covenant was not sealed until Christ was crucified (Matt. 26:28), it was under the Old Covenant that God anointed Jesus with the Holy Spirit (Luke 3:21-22) that He might be qualified to "preach the gospel . . . to heal the brokenhearted, to preach deliverance to the captives, and recovering of sight to the blind, to set at liberty them that are bruised" (Luke 4:16-21), and that He might "[go] about doing good, and healing all that were oppressed of the devil" (Acts 10:38).

Thus it was primarily for an energizing, practical purpose that the Holy Spirit was given under the Old Covenant. However, in a secondary way, it was also for an ethical, moral, spiritual purpose that He came to men. A few passages identify this. Probably it is most apparent in David's penitential prayer, "Do not cast me away from Thy presence, and do not take Thy Holy Spirit from me. Restore to me the joy of Thy salvation, and sustain me with a willing spirit. Then I will teach transgressors Thy ways, and sinners will be converted to Thee" (Ps. 51:11-13, NASB).

The enrichment of King Saul's life is another occasion. Samuel anointed him, declaring,

> The Spirit of the Lord will come upon thee, and thou shalt prophesy with them, and shall be turned into another man. And let it be, when these signs are come unto thee, that thou do as occasion serves thee; for God is with thee. And thou shalt go down before me to Gilgal; and, behold, I will come down unto thee, to offer burnt offerings, and to sacrifice sacrifices of peace offerings; seven days shalt thou tarry, till I come to thee, and shew thee what thou shalt do. And it was so, that when he had turned his back to go from Samuel, God gave him another heart: and all those signs came to pass that day. . . . And the Spirit of God came upon him (1 Sam. 10:6-10).

Also, in the early days of history God had warned the

generation of Noah, "My spirit shall not always strive with man" (Gen. 6:3).

There were those in addition who, from their place under the Old Covenant, foresaw an expanded ministry of the Holy Spirit *in an age to come*. Ezekiel, for example, proclaimed:

> I will take you out of the nations; I will gather you from all the countries and bring you back into your own land. I will sprinkle clean water on you, and you will be clean; I will cleanse you from all your impurities and from all your idols. I will give you a new heart and put a new spirit in you; I will remove from you your heart of stone and give you a heart of flesh. And I will put my Spirit in you and move you to follow my decrees and be careful to keep my laws (Ezek. 36:24-27, NIV).

Isaiah (32:15-17) and Joel (2:28-32), elsewhere quoted, are among others who made such predictions. A great day with the Holy Spirit was coming!

Under the New Covenant, new relationships with the Holy Spirit were established which had been only foreshadowed under the old. Is it not significant that the writer of Hebrews declared, "These all, having obtained a good report through faith, received not the promise: God having provided some better thing for us, that they without us should not be made perfect" (Heb. 11:39-40)?

1. The Twofold Purpose of the Holy Spirit

The energizing purpose of the Holy Spirit is continued under the New Covenant. With the baptism of the Holy Spirit, God promises and provides power (Acts 1:8). He is not satisfied with Christians who are weaklings. Gifts are bestowed "for the perfecting of the saints, for the work of the ministry, for the edifying of the body of Christ" (Eph. 4:12). The Holy Spirit comes for the practical purpose of preparing man to be useful to God.

But, in a marked sense, He particularly comes for the ethical purpose of developing Christlikeness, of cleansing, of baptizing the heart with love, of maturing character as predicted by Ezekiel. This purpose has taken the dominating position under the New Covenant relationship.

2. The Holy Spirit's Presence with All Believers

Although some Christians are spiritual (Spirit-filled)—"Ye that are spiritual" (Gal. 6:1)—and some are not—"I could not speak to you as unto spiritual" (1 Cor. 3:1)—yet even the unspiritual "have" the Holy Spirit. Paul wrote to the Corinthian church, "Know ye not that your body is the temple of the Holy Ghost which is in you, which ye have of God, and ye are not your own?" (1 Cor. 6:19). Under the new dispensation the Holy Spirit comes to and is *now present* with all believers. As Paul expressed it to the church in Rome, "If any man have not the Spirit of Christ, he is none of his" (Rom. 8:9).

This is not at all surprising since, as has been noted, the Holy Spirit, as the Administrator of the Godhead, has very actively dealt with the person in bringing him to Christ. He earnestly invited him to new life in Christ (Rev. 22:17), brought him under conviction for his sins (John 16:8-11), led him into justification (1 Cor. 6:11), regeneration (John 3:5-8), adoption (Gal. 4:4-7), and initial sanctification (1 Cor. 1:2; 6:9-11).

However, there is a difference between the Holy Spirit *being present* with the believer and His *filling* and *baptizing* him. God wants His temple filled!

3. The Availability of the Spirit

Christians are not automatically filled with the Spirit. Far too many never become so filled! Thus the command to all believers, "Be filled with the Spirit" (Eph. 5:18).

The Holy Spirit is *now available* to all believers *in a new and different way* than under the Old Covenant. This was intimated by Jesus when He told His disciples, "He dwelleth with you, and shall be in you" (John 14:17).

a. He is available in His fullness.

Near the end of His ministry, Jesus had an important public announcement to make. He chose a startling way to present it. It was the last, the eighth day of the Feast of the Tabernacles—the "greatest" day. In a stately, symbolic fashion the procession of priests was filing past with pitchers of water drawn from the pool of Siloam, to pour them out at the base of the altar of burnt offering as a reminder of the time when God gave water to the thirsty multitude in the wilderness. All this was to the chanting of Isaiah's words, "Ho, every one that thirsteth, come ye to the waters" (55:1), and, "With joy shall ye draw water out of the wells of salvation" (12:3). It was a solemn, tense moment.

Then, without warning, Jesus mounted a raised promontory in the Temple court and shouted out in a manner demanding attention from a suddenly quieted crowd:

"If a man is thirsty, let him come to me and drink. Whoever believes in me, as the Scripture has said, streams of living water will flow from within him." By this he meant the Spirit, whom those who believed in him were later to receive. Up to that time the Spirit had not been given, since Jesus had not yet been glorified (John 7:37-39, NIV).

Two or three things are to be noted. In Him and in Him alone was satisfaction for the thirsty soul. Again, for the believer there would be available a supply of this water in such an overabundant measure that it might be compared to an ever-flowing stream, gushing forth from the inner life for the benefit of others. We accommodate Him, not as a vessel, but as a channel through which He would flow to others. An understanding of this is basic.

To those listening this must have been a puzzling announcement. They did not recall any prophet or apostle who used such extravagant language as this. Isaiah (32:15-17), Ezekiel (36:24-27), Joel (2:28-32) had written about a pouring out of God's Spirit upon all flesh, about putting His spirit within, but nothing with this overflowing fullness. It was John who commented many years later as he wrote this account that this fulness was to be available *only after Jesus was glorified.* Pentecost, mused John from his point of observation, was the fulfillment of this possibility, and Pentecost followed the Ascension.

Turner has observed in his commentary on the Gospel of John, "In chapter 4, the Spirit which Jesus gives is likened to a well-spring of water (cf. Jer. 2:13; 17:13). But in chapter 7 the figure is much more bold; the spring becomes a river and is adequate not only for the individual consumption, but for all." And again, "It has occurred to many commentators that the well of water in chapter 4 implies the birth of the Spirit, while the rivers of water of chapter 7 implies that Spirit-filled and empowered life which has an outflow for others, so that the believer becomes a channel of blessing. ... The progression is noteworthy—from being born of the Spirit (3:5) to being filled with the Spirit (7:38). The Spirit-filled life is normative for the Christian" (Eph. 5:18).[1]

The poet has caught something of this message in the chorus:

> *Channels only, blessed Master,*
> *But with all Thy wondrous power*
> *Flowing through me, Thou canst use me*
> *Every day and every hour.*

b. The Holy Spirit is available to God's children upon request.

This announcement followed the other by a short interval of days, perhaps weeks. This was made, however, only to His disciples. They had asked Him to teach them to pray. He gave them that prayer known as the Lord's Prayer. He continued with the parable of the urgent midnight request by the householder which finally brought the needed bread for the unexpected guest. He then admonished them in their prayers to ask, seek, and knock. The present imperative tense describes persistent, continued action—"keep on asking, keep on seeking, keep on knocking" (NASB, margin). He reminded them that a father will not give an evil gift to his needy children—such as a stone when the request was for bread, such as a serpent when the need was a fish, such as a scorpion when the petition was for an egg. And this led to the pinnacle of His teaching. "If ye then being evil, know how to give good gifts unto your children, how much more shall your heavenly Father give the Holy Spirit to them that ask him?" (Luke 11:13).

If the former announcement was perplexing, this one was utterly startling. Did not the Holy Spirit always make His own sovereign choice upon whom He would come? Had that not been so from the very beginning of time? Samson had not requested the presence of the Spirit. Gideon was surpised when the Holy Spirit came upon him at the valley of Jezreel. Certainly Balaam must have been astounded when the Spirit chose to fill and qualify him. Who would have the boldness and the courage to ask God for the Holy Spirit? The disciples must have been overwhelmed and confounded.

But this promise, too, was under the new dispensation, the age of the Holy Spirit. Jesus would have His people to be aware that the Holy Spirit was available when He was "called alongside"—though not so unless the call be urgent, earnest, and insistent. This is why He later termed

Him the Paraclete—the "one-called-alongside." As a Friend He is available when summoned. The Father had promised.

This implies an *optional* relationship with the Spirit which is now open to the child of God under the New Covenant. And if it is optional, the relationship likewise is *volitional*. Furthermore, this speaks of *responsibility*. The believer is held responsible for the extent to which this relationship is established and maintained. Privilege spawns responsibility. Something monumental, astounding, explosive has now been opened to the believer—the experience of the fullness of the Spirit. This is the second revelation of significance which had been disclosed regarding the availability of the Spirit under the New Covenant.

There is no set pattern for the coming of the Spirit. His activity is not stereotyped. Jesus declared of Him, "The wind [Spirit] bloweth where it listeth, and thou hearest the sound thereof, but canst not tell whence it cometh, and whither it goeth: so is every one that is born of the Spirit" (John 3:8). May we not reverently add, "So is everyone who is baptized of the Spirit." As General Wiseman of the Salvation Army so aptly has remarked, "This is delightful, and seems to indicate that God's interventions cannot be stereotyped, but rather are replete with the grace of the unexpected."

4. Scripture Terms Describing This Effusion of the Holy Spirit

There are numerous New Testament descriptions or expressions of the coming of the Holy Spirit in His fullness to the believer under the New Covenant. In a broad sense they are synonymous and interchangeable. They are not necessarily listed herewith in order of their importance but in order of their first appearance:

To be "baptized with" the Holy Spirit—Matt. 3:11-17; Mark 1:8; Luke 3:16; John 1:33; Acts 1:5; 11:16; 1 Cor. 12:13

To "receive" the Holy Ghost—John 7:39; 14:17; 20:22; Acts 8:15, 17, 19; 10:47; 19:2; Gal. 3:2

To claim "the promise of the Father"—Luke 24:49; Acts 1:4; 2:39. (See also John 7:37-39; Luke 11:13.)

To have the Holy Ghost "come upon" you—Acts 1:8; 19:6

To be "filled with" the Holy Ghost—Acts 2:4; 4:31; 9:17; 13:52

I will "pour out" of my Spirit—Acts 2:17-18; 10:45

The "gift" of the Holy Ghost—Acts 2:38; 5:32; 8:18; 10:45; 11:17; 15:8; 2 Tim. 1:6-7

The Holy Ghost has "fallen upon" them—Acts 8:16; 10:44; 11:15

Thus it will be apparent that there are numerous records, far beyond that of the second chapter of Acts, of the fulfillment of Christ's prediction and the Father's promise of the Holy Spirit coming in His fullness upon His people.

5. The Question of Baptism with the Holy Spirit as an Initial Experience

There are those who maintain that this "baptism with the Holy Spirit" is an *initial* experience, common to all believers, received at the time of conversion. There are, however, numerous persuasive evidences against this view.

a. There is the rather convincing evidence of example. The Corinthian church, although possessing the Spirit (1 Cor. 6:19), was not Spirit-filled, or spiritual (1 Cor. 3:1). Even today, unfortunately, there are many professing Christians who, likewise, are not Spirit-filled, but are carnal and worldly, needing a baptism, a filling with the Holy Spirit.

b. There is the announcement of first importance made by Jesus himself. The Holy Spirit cannot be "received" by the world, by unconverted persons. "The Spirit of truth; whom the world cannot receive, because it seeth him not, neither knoweth him" (John 14:17). On the other hand, He commanded His disciples, as believers, to "receive the Holy Ghost" (John 20:22)—a promise fulfilled after Jesus was glorified (John 7:39). But the world was not ready to receive the Spirit not only because it had not seen or known Him, but also because it was not ready to be sanctified (John 17:9, 17). It needed first to become saved. But the disciples were ready and so would all other believers be in the years to come (v. 20). This, too, was Jesus' statement.

Now the word for "receive," *lambano,* normally indicates active and volitional action. This may be understood by recognizing that it is translated "take" in Rev. 22:17, "Whosoever will, *let him take* the water of life freely" (italics added). Certainly Paul's question of the men in Ephesus recorded in Acts 19:2, "Have ye received the Holy Ghost since [or when] ye believed?" may be translated, "Did you reach out and take the Holy Spirit when He was offered to you as believers?"

Thus Jesus was making it crystal clear, by both inclusion and exclusion, that the baptism with the Holy Spirit or being filled with the Spirit is not for the unconverted, but is only for the believer. It is dependent on the prior experience of conversion, of becoming a child of God, and then of earnestly calling on one's spiritual Father (cf. Luke 11:9-10, 13).

c. Another evidence that the infusion of the Holy Spirit is not an initial experience but is subsequent to conversion is God's pattern worked out in the Early Church as recorded in the Book of Acts. A record of the actual pattern of experience must be given high credence, but, in the light of Jesus' definitions of divine policy, should not be surprising. The word "subsequent" speaks, not of the length of time interval, but of the order of occurrence: "following in time, or as a result." If subsequent, the question may be, "By how long?" The answer is, "God is ready when you are." There is a law of readiness. There is also a law of responsibility.

The following table is set up in order of occurrence of those occasions when the gift of the Spirit is specified. All indicate *subsequent* timing.

Acts 2:1-4—*The disciples on the day of Pentecost*

Their names were written in heaven (Luke 10:20). They had been accepted into the family of God (John 17:6-9). (See also Luke 9:1; John 15:3.) Although much was yet to be learned and acquired by these humble disciples, who can deny that, as believers (John 2:11), they were justified, regenerated men?

Acts 2:37-39—*The 3,000 converts*

It is not stated specifically that they actually received the Holy Spirit, but strongly implied by the spiritual warmth of the church (Acts 2:41-47). But this was only after they became believers (John 14:17) and obeyed Peter's exhortation (Acts 2:38).*

Acts 4:31—*Many of those other 5,000 believers (4:4)*

Nothing is said of their receiving the Spirit when they believed, but many of them must have been present at that subsequent prayer meeting.

---

*There is a tendency to interpret "shall receive" (Acts 2:38) as a *predictive future*, in which sense it might well be translated "will receive" as in NIV. However, as given in KJV and NASB, "shall receive," may it not be accepted as an *imperative future*, requiring an exertion of the will, and that in line with 37, "What shall we do?" and with Luke 10:27, "Thou shalt love the Lord thy God with all thy heart"? This would agree with the active and volitional nature of the verb "receive" *(lambano*, v. 38), and with our Lord's admonition to an agressive, volitional act on the part of the believer in "asking," "seeking," "knocking" to receive the Spirit (Luke 11:9-13). Furthermore, the present tense in Acts 2:40 indicates that Peter *continued* to "exhort," which would refer to an imperative.

Acts 8:17—*The Samaritans*

A clear case. They had believed, and been baptized, but "as yet the Spirit was fallen on none of them."

Acts 9:1-18—*Saul of Tarsus*

To some this appears to be an immediate filling, as part of his conversion. But there are compelling reasons indicating otherwise. Saul, in a conciliatory prayer, immediately (and twice) called Jesus "Lord." Ananias three days later immediately addressed him by the believer's title, "Brother Saul." Again, Paul's conversion has always been known as a "Damascus-Road experience," not as a "Street-Called-Straight experience." Paul's longer account as given before Agrippa (Acts 26:12-19) really establishes this. Here Paul testifies to the very commission he received on the Damascus Road, clearly indicating his own spiritual redemption at that time. He finally declared to Agrippa, "Whereupon, O king Agrippa, I was not disobedient unto the heavenly vision: but shewed first unto them of Damascus, and at Jerusalem, and throughout all the coasts of Judaea, and then to the Gentiles, that they should repent and turn to God, and do works meet for repentance."

Acts 10:44—*Cornelius and his household*

The NASB, accurately rendering the aorist participle in 11:17, says: "God therefore gave to them the same gift as He did to us also *after believing* in the Lord Jesus Christ." A case where the sequence identifies "subsequent."

Acts 13:48-52—*The disciples*

The verb "were filled" is imperfect tense, and can properly be translated "and the disciples *continued to be full* of joy and the Holy Spirit" (Williams, italics added here and below). But we suggest it is clearly preferable to consider this as identical to the translation of a parallel passage, Acts 8:17, as *an imperfect of repeated action:* "Then they laid their hands upon them, and *one by one* they received the Holy Ghost" (Williams; cf. Luke 14:7 and John 19:3). Thus the text would read: "The disciples, *one by one*, were being filled with joy, and with the Holy Ghost." It thus would describe an interesting process of the ongoing ministry of the Holy Spirit among the believers of the Early Church, an instructive passage regarding post-conversion baptisms with the Spirit as He moved among them in His duties as the Administrator of the Godhead.

Acts 19:1-7—*The 12 disciples in Ephesus*

Although disputed by some, the evidence is convincing. "Disciples," unless associated with a person, like "disciples of John," always indicates in Scripture disciples of Christ. Their lack of knowledge regarding the Spirit is only too common, even today, among believers. The question is significant. Paul knew that there were disciples in those days too who, though believers, had not yet received the Holy Spirit. It was an evangelistic challenge to believers then, as it should be now: "Have *you* received the Holy Spirit?"

d. A further evidence that the baptism with the Holy Spirit was not an initial experience at the time of conversion in the Early Church is that, while there are these several instances where He was given, yet there are at least twice as many accounts of conversion when *no mention at all* is made of the Holy Spirit being poured out upon them. Why should the Spirit be identified in these several instances but not in all if the baptism with the Spirit was enjoyed as an initial experience by all?

The pattern of conversion is set in Acts 2:47: "The Lord added to the church daily such as should be saved." The individual accounts, as examples, specify that they "believed" (4:4); "believers were the more added to the Lord" (5:14); many were "obedient to the faith" (6:7); "a great number . . . turned to the Lord" (11:21); they "believed and were baptized" (18:8). But that they were also filled with the Spirit is only occasionally declared.

e. Another evidence that receiving the Holy Spirit in

the Early Church was a subsequent experience is an inference. Acts 6:1-3 records that it was necessary to institute a "search" to find "seven men . . . full of the Holy Ghost . . . whom we may appoint" to care for the neglected widows. A search had to be made. This indicates that church members were not all Spirit-filled then, either. Likewise Barnabas is set apart among believers as "a good man" and "full of the Holy Ghost" (11:22-24). Being filled with the Spirit was the desirable, indeed the natural experience for the child of God—even as it is now—but the Christians did not all then and, unfortunately do not now, attain to it.

There is another evidence, related to the attitude of Jesus, which will be explored later. But, for the moment let us consider the case of some students of the Word who approach the matter differently. They would detach baptism with the Spirit from the other terms, then declare that the baptism is an initial experience, but that it does not always include being filled with the Spirit, or receiving the Spirit. It is held that these may mark a subsequent experience.

This approach, however, does violence to the obvious connection made by Jesus himself among these terms. Very clearly, with Him, the promise of the Father (Acts 1:4), which was not only to the 12, but to all believers of all generations and peoples (Acts 2:39), the baptism with the Spirit (1:5), the Holy Spirit coming upon you (1:8), and being filled with the Spirit (2:4) are one and the same experience, whether initial or subsequent. Peter recognized this to be true (Acts 11:15-17). It also fails to note the difference between those who "have" the Spirit and thus are "born" of the Spirit, and those who "receive" Him and thus are "baptized" with Him. Furthermore, baptism is a penetrating, saturating experience (Acts 8:38-39), whether in water or in the Holy Spirit (11:16).

6. The Case of 1 Cor. 12:13

On first reading, this verse appears to be contrary both to other scriptures and to the experience of the Early Church as recorded in the Book of Acts. There are those who hold that it declares that every Chrisitan who *comes into the church* is baptized into the body of Christ through the baptism with the Spirit, thus making such a baptism an initial experience, common to all Christians. Now when one verse appears to contradict the general flow of Scripture, an examination is in order.

Here are two excerpts from the passage as quoted from the NIV:

> The body is a unit, though it is made up of many parts; and though all its parts are many, they form one body. So it is with Christ. For we were all baptized by one Spirit into one body—whether Jews or Greeks, slave or free—and we were all given the one Spirit to drink ... so that there should be no division in the body (1 Cor. 12:12-13, 25).
> Now you are the body of Christ, and each one of you is a part of it (1 Cor. 12:27).

a. There is a *contrast of persons* written into this passage. Note the emphasized, personalized pronouns—the "we" of verse 13 and the "you" of verse 27. In Greek the personal pronoun in the nominative case is included in the verb. When the pronoun is used it is for emphasis. When two such pronouns are used in the same passage it is for contrast—a common and important practice. Paul uses the contrast dramatically in the same letter: "*We* are fools for Christ's sake, but *ye* are wise in Christ; *we* are weak, but *ye* are strong; *ye* are honourable, but *we* are despised" (1 Cor. 4:10). The writers of the Gospels use it in comparing the baptisms of John and Jesus: "*I* indeed baptize you with water unto repentance: but he that cometh after me is mightier than I . . . *he* shall baptize you with

111

the Holy Ghost" (Matt. 3:11; Mark 1:8; Luke 3:16). This is true even in widely separated verses as in John 18:31, 38; 19:6. "Take *ye* him and judge him . . . *I* find in him no fault . . . Take *ye* him; for *I* find no fault in him."*

Then who are the "we" of verse 13, and the "you" of verse 27 who are in contrast? The "you" of verse 27 are the believers who make up the church in Corinth—"the body of Christ, and each one of you a part of it" (NIV). They had been accepted into the church on the very terms Jesus himself had set for such membership: "The Lord added to the church daily such as should be saved" (Acts 2:47). For "Many of the Corinthians hearing believed, and were baptized" (Acts 18:8). And it is specifically mentioned that the Holy Spirit had taken up His abode in their hearts (1 Cor. 6:19). But, it is just as specifically stated that they were not "spiritual" Christians (3:1), not Spirit-filled, not baptized with the Spirit. And their mode of life bore that out, in carnality, childishness, envying, strife, divisiveness.

In contrast, the "we" of verse 13 are also believers, but believers who additionally have been baptized with, have received, the Spirit, indeed, who have been "made to drink" of, and were, manifestly, filled with the Spirit. This, according to Jesus (John 14:17 and 20:22), and according to the universal experience of the Early Church was an experience reserved for the believer subsequent to his conversion.

*Italics have been added in each quotation to point up the contrasting pronouns. Other examples of contrast are: Matt. 8:7, 9; Luke 22:32; John 4:38; 5:35; 7:8; 8:13-15; 8:23; 8:41, 44; 13:33; 15:5, 16; 16:7; Acts 9:5; 22:8; 26:15; 13:33; 1 Cor. 1:12; 3:4; Col. 1:17, 18, 25, 28; Heb. 1:5; 5:5; James 2:3; 1 John 4:4, 5, 6; 4:19. The use of two personal pronouns in the same passage is always for contrast, and sometimes with important insights, as may be noted in the above incidents. However, unfortunately, no translation has found a way of imparting this subtle information.

Thus here the *hemeis* ("we") of verse 13 is in contrast with the *humeis* ("you") of verse 27. The contrast is simply between believers who have been baptized and filled with the Holy Spirit, and those who have not. That makes the difference.

But who are the "we *all?*" An examination of the verse will indicate that the "all" are not all *individuals*, but are all *types* of Christians—all nationalities "whether Jews or Gentiles"; all strata of society "whether bond or free." God is no respecter of persons in the baptism with the Holy Spirit. As Peter said on the Day of Pentecost, "The promise [of the gift of the Holy Spirit] is unto you, and to your children [all generations], and to all that are afar off [all nations and types of believers], even as many as the Lord our God shall call" (Acts 2:39).

b. There is also an identification of *purpose.* Note that the central theme of the passage is not an entrance into "*the* body" of Christ, but into "*one* body." The body should be "a unity"—"one." "There should be no division in the body." In diversity, illustrated by the diverse members of a body (vv. 12-27), there is unity *if the unifying force of the Holy Spirit knits it together.*

Therefore, this baptism of the Spirit is not into *the* body, or establishing *membership* in the church, but into *one* body or establishing *unity* within the church. Membership in the body of Christ came to *us*, implies Paul, in the same way as to *you* Corinthians, through faith and acceptance. Unity, however, came to *us*, in spite of our diverse background and origin, through the cleansing, sanctifying baptism of the one Spirit.

Here was a cleverly devised charge by Paul to a schismatic church to come into the harmony, the oneness, enjoyed by so many others through the baptism and filling with the Holy Spirit. It was an experience enjoyed by

Spirit-filled believers of all types, Jew and Gentile, slave or master. "Come into that fellowship," he invited.

c. An outcome of this baptism would be unity. This was at the heart of Christ's prayer recorded in John 17, "May they be brought to complete unity" (v. 23, NIV). Paul now declares what Christ's prayer implied—that this can be accomplished by a baptism with the Spirit. It was a particularly appropriate emphasis in a church of widely diverse membership in which the seeds of division were obvious.

Charles W. Carter, in the *Wesleyan Bible Commentary,* has made a cogent observation on this verse:

> In the previous section Paul has emphasized the variety of spiritual gifts. He now emphasizes the unity within that variety. The Corinthian church prided itself in its great variety of gifts. It had little to boast about in its unity. Paul seeks to show that without the unity the multiplication of gifts is meaningless.
>
> The human body serves to illustrate the principle of unity in the body of Christ (v. 12). No member, of itself, constitutes the body. Nor will all the members, unless properly related one to the other in the body, constitute a body. The body is more than the sum of its parts—it is a body—an emergent from the proper relation and harmony of all the parts, even as water is an emergent of H_2O. Water is something more than H_2O. It is water, and if it is reduced to its chemical components, it ceases to be water. The spiritual body, the body of Christ—the church—is like that. It is only the Church when the members are harmoniously related and functioning in unison. This is made possible by the living soul of the Church—the Holy Spirit.
>
> *The Church is made a spiritual body through the baptism in the Spirit.* Through that glorious baptism Jews and Greeks, slaves and freemen, women and men, wise and simple, rich and poor, are all made one in the body of Christ—each in his respective place and fulfilling his respective function—because each has become a partaker of the spiritual water of life (cf. John 7:37-39).[2]

The oneness, repeatedly prayed for by Jesus for His Church (John 17), will be achieved only when Christians are sanctified (John 17:17) through the one baptism which is uniquely Christian, the baptism with the Holy Spirit (Acts 1:4-5).

d. The question of whether the Holy Spirit is the Agent or the Medium in the baptism is raised by the use of the word "by"—"By one Spirit are we all baptized." This is the translation in the KJV, NASB, and the NIV—this in spite of the fact that *en,* when associated with baptism, is everywhere else universally translated "with" or "in" (see Acts 1:5; Matt. 3:11; Mark 1:8; Luke 3:1). Thus the usual translation makes water, or the Holy Spirit, to be the element or *Medium* with which one is baptized, either by John or by Jesus as the *Agent,* the one who does the baptizing. But it provides no *medium* or element with which the Holy Spirit would baptize, and leaves the statement incomplete, if not incomprehensible and confusing.

Now, if one is willing to concede that the correct translation is "with" or "in," as does NEB, RSV, Weymouth, Goodspeed, and NASB margin, then the Holy Spirit is the *Medium* or element, and Christ is understood to be the *Agent* who does the baptizing, as in all other instances. The statement, then, becomes meaningful. Indeed, this agrees with Paul's declaration in Eph. 4:4-5, "There is . . . one Lord, one faith, one baptism." For we agree with Ralph Earle, as quoted elsewhere more fully: "The only distinctive and utterly Christian baptism is the baptism with the Holy Spirit. That cannot be duplicated by any other religion. It is peculiarly Christ's. '*He* shall baptize you with the Holy Spirit' " (Mark 1:8).[3]

8/

JESUS AND THE BAPTISM WITH THE HOLY SPIRIT

Possibly the most telling evidence of all, indicating that the baptism with the Holy Spirit is not an initial experience but is available only after conversion, is related to Jesus' treatment of the subject as a whole. For in His teaching ministry, He started, not with the baptism of the Spirit, but with sanctification by the Spirit.

Jesus had heard John announce that the baptism by Him would not be with water, but with the Holy Spirit (Matt. 3:11-17). But Jesus did not then discuss the matter himself. Months passed by, growing into years.

1. Prayer for the Disciples

It was the evening before the Crucifixion. Gathered

with His disciples, and following the Last Supper with them, Jesus had an ardent session of prayer with His Father as recorded in John 17. The subject of His prayer was varied, including unity of the Church, separation from the world, joy in His followers. But the heart of it was sanctification. "Sanctify them," He prayed, "through the truth" (v. 17). And who was "them"? Observe how specific He was. "Not the world" (v. 9), He said. Without question many times He had prayed for the world, had agonized for its salvation and interceded for its reconciliation with a forgiving God. But not now. Thus was established an exclusion, not by oversight, not by omission, but by direct announcement and that by Jesus himself. The sinful world was not ready and is not now ready to be sanctified; it must first be saved. At this moment His intercession was not for the world but for His disciples, men who already belonged to God and to Him (vv. 7-10). They needed not to be saved, but to be sanctified.

Thus, since the beneficiaries of this prayer were to be believers and *only* believers, it was not initial sanctification to which He was referring. That had been accomplished at the time of conversion by the presence of the Holy Spirit. See 1 Cor. 1:2 and 6:9-11 for an example of initial sanctification, which lacked entire sanctification in cleansing results (3:1-4; cf. 2 Cor. 7:1).

It was not progressive sanctification. That would have been recorded in a present tense imperative indicating continued action, as in Luke 11:9, "Keep asking, keep seeking, keep knocking" (NASB margin). This request was in the aorist tense, the imperative of the immediate point action of an event.

And why this urgency, this earnestness, this undisguised concern for the sanctification of these regenerate men?

It was within hours of His leaving this world, and these men were not yet ready to carry out the gospel which He was purchasing with His blood. He was painfully aware of their self-seeking, their material-mindedness, their desire to be recognized. The mother of James and John, undoubtedly with their approval if not actual encouragement, had recently brought her two sons before Jesus, boldly requesting that they should sit, one on the right and the other on the left hand "in His glory" when His kingdom should be established. Repeatedly, the latest occasion being that very evening at the Last Supper, there had been heated disputes among the disciples as to who was "the greatest" among them. And earlier that evening pride had forbidden them to wash one another's feet at the Passover meal until Jesus himself performed the menial task.

On a previous occasion James and John had noticed that the Samaritans did not receive Jesus because He was travelling toward Jerusalem and, in a vindictive mood, they had asked permission to "command fire to come down from heaven, and consume them." These men lacked compassion, they had no real sense of conviction, and showed impotence in the face of the needs of the people. They also proved to be cowardly in the face of danger—even to the extent of Peter's thrice-expressed denial.

These men were not ready to be His witnesses, His messengers, His apostles. They exhibited the debilitating sins of the spirit. They needed to be sanctified, and that right now.

2. Prayer for All Believers

For whom else did Jesus pray in that memorable High Priestly prayer? The answer is not hard to find. He prayed for Christians, believers, His Church. "Neither pray I for these alone," He continued in v. 20, "but for them also which shall believe on me through their word." His Church, His believers of today, have needs comparable to those of the disciples. They too "come short" and need the power of the Holy Spirit and the cleansing of their hearts to become overcomers.

Vanity, anger, gossip, pride are matched with lack of love, grieving the Spirit, failure to read the Word; compounded with resentment, an unforgiving spirit, touchiness; added to timidity, fear, coldness of spirit. The hearts of all persons, even though believers, need cleansing, need the sanctification for which Jesus prayed, whatever their tongue, their culture, their country.

Truly the believer of today was included in that prayer of our Lord. For, no less than in that day, our Lord today desperately needs witnesses, soul winners, men and women of conviction, of power, of purity of heart, of burdened compassion.

3. Calvary

And upon what confidence did Jesus thus pray? Because He was giving His life, not just for the sinful world that it might not perish, not just for the sinners who needed to be forgiven, for those who needed a new birth, for those outside the family of God who needed to be adopted into His family. This was but part of the purpose of Calvary, as declared in John 3:16.

But "Christ also loved the *church*"—the children of God, the saved—"and gave himself for it, that he might sanctify and cleanse it" (Eph. 5:25-26).

What an awe-inspiring thought! He gave himself not only that I might be saved, but that I might be sanctified. His sacrifice, His suffering, His cry of dereliction—"My God, my God, why hast *thou* forsaken me?"—was no greater in order that the sinful world might be rescued from its depth of sin, than His suffering in order that those having received such a wonderful salvation might be sanctified. And His burden today is just as keen that His Church, His believers, might indeed be sanctified, as it is that the sinful world, the heathen world, be saved. Can I treat lightly the import of this complete purpose of His death, this full accomplishment on the Cross?

4. The Holy Spirit

And what was the *means* by which our Lord would accomplish this? It was not until immediately after His resurrection that He made this plain. He introduced it by advising the disciples to wait for "the promise of the Father, which ye have heard of me," and continued with, "John truly baptized with water: but ye shall be baptized with the Holy Ghost not many days hence" (Acts 1:4-5).

This they did. And they were gathered together "in prayer and supplication" when it happened.

"Suddenly . . . they were all filled with the Holy Ghost" (Acts 2:2-4), "baptized with the Holy Ghost" (Acts 11:15-17). It had occurred as an event, in a moment of time, even as Jesus had requested in the aorist tense of point action (John 17:17). The Administrator of the Triune God had suddenly come in all His fullness.

5. The Sanctified Church of the First Century

The immediate result of the disciples' being baptized with the Holy Spirit was that they were truly sanctified (1 Thess. 5:23) on that Day of Pentecost. They were changed men. Instead of fear there was boldness. Instead of self-interest there was power. Instead of vindictiveness there was love. Instead of weakness there was Christian compassion and concern. They shared their goods with the needy, their joy with the sorrowing, their confidence one in another. Divisiveness was suddenly engulfed in the significant, oft-repeated phrase unique to the Book of Acts—"with one accord."

This revolutionary spirit of liberation and of dynamic outreach was by no means limited to the Eleven. It was to about 120 that this experience was confirmed on the Day of Pentecost. And immediately and repeatedly it became apparent among the additional throngs of those who "should believe through their word." The principle was established for all believers, both then and now. As Paul later expressed it for the child of God, "This is the will of God, even your sanctification." A careful study of the Book of Acts reveals that again and again this miracle of sanctifying grace was repeated in the hearts of believers by the effusion of the Spirit.

Peter's description in Acts 15 set the pattern for what was happening when the Spirit came down upon believers in the Early Church. "Men and brethren, ye know how that a good while ago God made choice among us, that the Gentiles by my mouth should hear the word of the gospel, and believe." And many did hear him and were saved. Peter continued, "And [or then] God, which knoweth the hearts, bare them witness, giving them the Holy Ghost, even as he did unto us." Aorist tense participles identify the crisis point action of the gift—the "giving" and the "purifying." As with the disciples, the gift of the Spirit and the cleansing of the hearts were immediate transactions, decisive acts related one to the other—"even as he did unto us."

This precise account of immediate cleansing would apply to the Samaritans when they "received" the Holy Spirit (Acts 8:17) as well as to the household of Cornelius when the Spirit "fell on them" (Acts 10:44), "baptized them" (Acts 11:16). It would apply also to the others of the 120 who were filled on the Day of Pentecost (Acts 2), to the new converts (4:4) many of whom were undoubtedly later filled with the Holy Spirit (4:31), to Saul on the street called Straight when he was "filled with" the Holy Spirit (9:18), to the many disciples included in the account of 13:52 when one by one they "were filled with joy and the Holy Spirit," to the 12 disciples in Ephesus when the Holy Spirit "came on" them (19:6). It was the pattern of entire sanctification falling on the Early Church.

However, this was not a universal experience. Jesus had said of the promise of the Father, "How much more will the heavenly Father give the Holy Spirit to them that ask" (Luke 11:13). Unfortunately, His children did not all ask, or they did not ask with necessary zeal (Luke 11:9) even as there were many of His countrymen who did not "receive" Jesus (John 1:11-12). As has been noted elsewhere there are many cases of conversion listed in the Book of Acts without evidence that to them "the gift of the Spirit" was given. Apparently they were satisfied with His *presence*, and didn't ask for His *fullness*.

There was indeed at least one church, the Corinthians, who *remained* unspiritual, carnal, divided—presumably because they didn't ask. That they "believed and were baptized" is recorded in Acts 18:8, and therefore they were among the throngs of converts who were added to the Church by the Lord (Acts 2:47). That they enjoyed the presence of the Holy Spirit is evident from 1 Cor. 6:19, "Your body is the temple of the Holy Ghost." But that they sought out "the promise of the Father" or "were baptized with the Holy Spirit" is not recorded. Indeed, Paul identifies them as being *not* "spiritual," but rather as being childish, carnal, divisive, quarreling (1 Cor. 1:1-11; 3:1-4), needing total cleansing (2 Cor. 7:1).

6. The Sanctified 20th-Century Church

And what says this today to the Church and to the individual Christian? It says that this effusion of the Holy Spirit, this sanctifying act of the Spirit, is still today a Blood-bought privilege, to them that ask; that Christ yearns to bestow the same experience of sanctification; that surely He even now continues His prayer before the Father for His children—"Sanctify them!"

And, praise God, His prayer is being answered! Around the world, wherever this message of heart cleansing and Spirit filling is proclaimed, God is consistently fulfilling His promise, His provision, His prayer—to those who earnestly ask.

The infilling of the Holy Spirit as a subsequent experience for the believer *is real.* His sanctifying presence and power *are genuine.* God the Holy Spirit *is moving!*

All over the world, the Spirit is moving;
All over the world, as the prophet said it would be;
All over the world, there's a mighty revelation
*Of the glory of the Lord as the waters cover the sea.**

---

*"The earth shall be filled with the knowledge of the glory of the Lord, as the waters cover the sea" (Hab. 2:14).

9/

SPIRIT BAPTISM AS A CHRISTIAN TERM

1. A Unique Christian Rite

The term "baptized with or in the Spirit" has been frequently referred to in this volume. It has been noted that it was introduced by John the Baptist, as recorded by Matthew (3:11-14):

> I indeed baptize you with water unto repentance: but he that cometh after me is mightier than I, whose shoes I am not worthy to bear: he shall baptize you with the Holy Ghost, and with fire. . . . Then cometh Jesus from Galilee to Jordan unto John, to be baptized of him. But John forbad him, saying, I have need to be baptized of thee, and comest thou to me?

Clearly John saw Jesus as his superior, and Jesus' baptism as of far greater importance than his. Indeed, if he had had his way there would have been a baptism, right then, of himself by Jesus, not in water but with the Holy Spirit. But, of course, that was not to be. As the Apostle John later put it, "The Holy Ghost was not yet given; because that Jesus was not yet glorified" (John 7:39). Only after the suffering, resurrection, and ascension of Jesus was the baptism with the Holy Spirit to be available to the believer.

Paul gave reference to Jesus' baptism of His followers with the Spirit when he wrote of "one Lord, one faith, one baptism" (Eph. 4:5), and when he declared, "By one Spirit are we all baptized" (1 Cor. 12:13). It is the only baptism which confers grace. In this its superiority was now recognized by John the Baptist, and later by Paul, 1 Cor. 1:17: "Christ sent me not to baptize, but to preach the gospel."

Ralph Earle's commentary on Mark 1:7-8, a parallel passage, is compelling:

> In view of the clear assertion of John the Baptist here, it is difficult to understand the almost universal neglect in the Christian Church of the baptism with the Holy Spirit. There was nothing particularly unique about John's method of water baptism. Judaism baptized new converts with water. Water baptism is thus not distinctively a *Christian* rite. The only distinctive and utterly unique Christian baptism is the baptism with the Holy Spirit. That cannot be duplicated by any other religion. It is peculiarly Christ's: *"He* shall baptize you with the Holy Spirit" (v. 8).[1]

Commissioner Samuel Logan Brengle's writings, as exemplified by *When the Holy Ghost Is Come*, are replete with statements about the baptism with the Spirit. "What patient, waiting, expectant faith reckons done, the baptism with the Holy Ghost actually accomplishes." And again, "The act of believing, is man's part; the act of baptizing with the Holy Ghost is God's part." And, once more, "The advocates of entire sanctification as an experience wrought in the soul by the baptism of the Holy Spirit subsequent to regeneration call it 'the second blessing.' "[2]

That old-time, able exponent of entire sanctification, C. W. Ruth, in a book by that title declares:

> Whoever is sanctified wholly has the baptism with the Holy Ghost; whoever has the baptism with the Holy Ghost is sanctified wholly. It is the baptism with the Holy Ghost that sanctifies wholly. These terms simply represent different phases of the same experience, and are used as synonyms . . . In Acts 15:8-9, we find that God gave to the house of Cornelius, under the preaching of Peter, exactly the same experience He had given the Apostles on the day of Pentecost . . . So we see clearly that the Pentecostal blessing—the baptism with the Holy Ghost—does not simply mean the empowering for service, but the *purifying of the heart by faith*. . . . The purifying of the heart and the sanctifying of the heart and the baptism with the Holy Ghost take place simultaneously.[3]

2. Born of the Spirit and Baptized with the Spirit

To some there is a confusion of identifying baptism with the Spirit with birth by the Spirit. H. Orton Wiley has a helpful analysis.

> There are certain other acts or functions of . . . [the Spirit's] administrative work which . . . pertain especially to the work of salvation, and may be classified broadly under two general heads—the Holy Spirit as "the Lord and Giver of Life," and the Holy Spirit as "a sanctifying Presence." To the former belongs the "birth of the Spirit" or the initial experience of salvation; to the latter, the "baptism with the Spirit"—a subsequent work by which the soul is made holy . . . known as entire sanctification.[4]

Indeed, there are two distinct experiences established by

the Scriptures—"saved" and "sanctified"; "born of the Spirit" and "baptized with the Spirit." The two should not be confused.

It has been observed that the New Testament does not repeatedly urge the believer to be baptized with the Holy Spirit. Neither does it repeatedly urge the sinner to be born again. However, did not Jesus' exhortation to Nicodemus, "Ye must be born again," constitute an exhortation to every sinner to realize this experience of the new birth?

And did not the directive of Jesus to His disciples to "receive the Spirit," to "wait for the promise of the Father," and His promise, "Ye shall be baptized with the Holy Ghost," penetrate through the years to "them also which shall believe on me through their word"? Peter quite evidently thought so when he declared on the day of Pentecost, "Ye shall receive the gift of the Holy Ghost. For the promise is unto you, and to your children, and to all that are afar off, even as many as the Lord our God shall call" (Acts 2:38-39).

3. God's Call to Holiness

Thus every exhortation given to the Church toward the experience of sanctification must be accepted also as an exhortation to be baptized with the Spirit—for that is how God planned that the experience shall be gained. The Holy Spirit is the Divine Executive for sanctification, whether it be initial or entire sanctification.

Paul's prayer for the exemplary believers in Thessalonica, "The very God of peace sanctify you wholly," was an invitation for them to be filled with the Spirit. His exhortation to the strife-torn church in Corinth, "Having therefore these promises, dearly beloved, let us cleanse ourselves from all filthiness of the flesh and spirit, perfecting holiness in the fear of God" (2 Cor. 7:1) was another way of urging them to receive the Holy Spirit in His fullness. This announcement to the believers in Ephesus that "Christ also loved the church, and gave himself for it; that he might sanctify and cleanse it" (Eph. 5:25-26) was another way of declaring to them that Christ desired, through the administrative office of the Holy Spirit, to accomplish in them that experience of entire sanctification. The writer of the Epistle to the Hebrews was, in his own way, declaring that God had provided an outpouring of the Spirit so that, through chastening, "we might be partakers of his holiness" (Heb. 12:10). Peter challenged those who had been "begotten again unto a lively hope by the resurrection of Jesus Christ from the dead" with the call: "As he which hath called you is holy, so be ye holy in all manner of conversation" (1 Pet. 1:15). He wrote this in the full knowledge and confidence that this was possible through a baptism with the Holy Spirit, as established on the Day of Pentecost in the realm of his own memory. And each one of these exhortations is marked by the aorist tense of an event.

Yes, every exhortation to holiness in the New Testament is a recognition of the possibility of a cleansing outpouring of the Holy Spirit to the believer who, in faith, asks, seeks, and knocks (Luke 11:9-13).

4. "Where It Listeth"

Now, while the cleansing power of the Holy Spirit's presence is established as a basic for sanctification, the manner of His coming, even the title attached to His coming, is varied in the New Testament records, and will vary among believers today.

To some He came with highly dramatic associations, as on the Day of Pentecost; to others in the quiet visit from a godly messenger, as to Paul in Damascus. On some occasions He came upon them as part of a mighty mass meeting, as in the prayer service of Acts 4:31; to others, during a quiet heart-searching, as to the Samaritans under the ministry of Peter and John recorded in Acts 8. To some it was in the home atmosphere, as with Cornelius; to others in a small gathering of God's children, as with the 12 disciples in Ephesus. To some the blessing came as a surprise even to those who ministered, as it was to the Jews in Caesarea (Acts 10:45); to others, in evident response to earnest prayer and petition, as in Ephesus.

The circumstances varied, and so did the terms used to describe the experience. Not all "were baptized with." Some "were filled with," some "received," others "claimed the promise of the Father." The Spirit "came upon" others, "was poured out upon" or "was fallen upon" still others. Terminology in the scripture records is interchangeable.

The principles of receiving the Holy Spirit remain the same—expectant prayer, sanctifying faith,* a receptive heart, total surrender on the part of the recipient, and a willingness and readiness on the part of God to baptize with the Spirit when He recognizes the sincerity of the seeker.

But a precise pattern? Really, not so. This can lead to artificial stimuli, to demands for certain signs from God, to a presumption of achievement based often on physical or even emotional signs.

Again we recall Jesus' reminiscence: "The wind bloweth where it listeth, and thou hearest the sound

---

*Sanctifying faith can be described in the same language as saving faith. It is that act of personal heart trust by which the seeker commits himself to God and accepts as his own the sanctification which God so freely offers.

The believing seeker looks to the same Savior, and kneels at the same Cross. He is inspired by the same act of Atonement, by the divine will and love it expresses, and by the grace and blessing that flow from it.

The Lord Jesus Christ, who was received as *justifying* Savior, is now received as *sanctifying* Saviour (Eph. 5:25-26).[5]

thereof, but canst not tell whence it cometh, and whither it goeth: so is every one that is born of the Spirit" (John 3:8). And, so it is with everyone that is baptized of the Spirit.

10/

EARTHEN VESSELS

Man is so created by God that he must find within himself a satisfactory relationship between the natural and the supernatural. In the Middle Ages, a troubled period of history, all was supernatural. Witchcraft, evil spirits, and devil possession were associated with every ill, physical and mental. Severe means—imprisonment, torture, flagellation, to the actual taking of life itself by burning at the stake—were the accepted means of cure or punishment.

The Renaissance of the 14th, 16th, and 17th centuries, with its brilliant cultural outbursts and the explosive power of new learning and education, laid the foundation for a sudden and sometimes violent reversal. Humanism reigned; the natural took over from the supernatural. Voltaire epitomized this era. He believed in God and called himself a theist. Yet his God did not intervene in the course of events. To him there was no Providence, no miracle, no divine revelation. Christ was left out of Voltaire's philosophical outlook; the Scriptures were vilified by his scorn; immortality counted but little, or was identified as a selfish illusion of man's pride. Voltaire's creed was natural religion—religion viewed as equivalent to morality and reduced to the self-evident truths of justice, goodness, and truth. The warmth of the Spirit had no place in Voltaire's theology. God's only advice to man could be: "Be just."

These two opposing views, the natural and the supernatural, must be reconciled. There is within mankind the natural; there is also within his heart the supernatural. Indeed, as Paul declares: "Do you not know that your body is a temple of the Holy Spirit who is in you, whom you have from God, and that you are not your own?" (1 Cor. 6:19, NASB). Indeed we have this treasure in "earthen vessels," to use Paul's term—and for a purpose.

> We have this treasure in earthen vessels, that the surpassing greatness of the power may be of God and not from ourselves; we are afflicted in every way, but not crushed; perplexed, but not despairing; persecuted, but not forsaken; struck down, but not destroyed; always carrying about in the body the dying of Jesus, that the life of Jesus also may be manifested in our body (2 Cor. 4:7-10, NASB).

The purpose of this "treasure" being possessed in "earthen vessels" is "that the surpassing greatness of the power may be of God and not from ourselves." He is exhibiting His greatness within our weakness. As Paul elsewhere declared: "Most gladly, therefore, I will rather boast about my weaknesses, that the power of Christ may dwell in me" (2 Cor. 12:9, NASB). And as the inimitable John the Baptist decreed: "He must increase, but I must decrease" (John 3:30).

The result of this being Spirit-possessed is a series of

contrasts and, to many, conflicts. The inward struggle may be severe, harsh, perplexing. Note *The Living Bible* translation of 2 Cor. 4:8-9:

> We are pressed on every side by troubles, but not crushed and broken. We are perplexed because we don't know why things happen as they do, but we don't give up and quit. We are hunted down, but God never abandons us. We get knocked down; but we get up again and keep going.

It is well, then, for the believer to learn to recognize these tension points, their cause and their cure.

1. Temptations

One of the most obvious tension points is that of temptation. There are Christians who suppose that to be Spirit-filled is to be free from temptation. How manifestly untrue. Fresh from the creative genius of God and created in the image and likeness of that God, Adam was tempted. Retaining the divinity of the Godhead, but clothed with the vulnerable humanity of mankind, Jesus was tempted "in all points like as we are," and undoubtedly much more severely than we ever may be. And this immediately after His anointing with the Holy Spirit. The most holy of God's children face temptation. It is the constant evidence that Satan never gives up his desire and effort to reclaim those who were once his.

One of the most frequently expressed questions which I have met in all parts of the world whether in Zaire or Canada, Japan or Rhodesia, Mexico or Korea—is this: "Is the Spirit-filled Christian free from temptation?" Our constant answer has been and must be, "No." But there is also the assurance that he is able to overcome temptation. He can and should be "more than conqueror through him that loved us."

2. Physical Limitations

"Earthen vessels" means physical limitations. Early the devoted Christian must learn that he is subject to these. Whether they mean merely physical weariness, fatigue, even exhaustion; or illness, failing health, a physical handicap—they all come to the Spirit-filled Christian. Indeed, he must come to respect his physical limitations and provide sufficient rest, recreation, and suitable food to compensate. God expects this of His people. But he must also be willing to accept that which seems unreasonable or undeserved. Men like Commissioner Samuel Brengle give eloquent testimony to the use God puts to earthen vessels which are limited in vitality, marred by injury or illness, worn by the very number of years accumulated in a long life.

3. Emotions

And what of the emotions of a Spirit-filled man? Should they not be quite different? Should they not be obviously spiritual—even Christlike? The answer is yes and no. Man is a creature of emotions. To deprive him of this would be to deprive him of his humanity. Love is one emotion. Love can be self-centered, grasping for attention, even judgmental. That is selfish love, not Christian love. The unselfish, compassionate love of Christ is an indispensable hallmark of the Spirit-filled man!

Anger is carnal when it is self-defensive. It is spiritual when it defends God, His purity and righteousness, His kingdom. Surely it was a godly anger which Jesus exhibited in overturning the money tables and in driving the merchants from His Father's house! Mark 3 records specifically an occasion of Christ's anger. A man with a withered hand was discovered by Jesus. The Pharisees kept watching Him closely to see if He would cure the cripple, for it was the Sabbath Day. It was then that Jesus "looked round about on them with anger, being grieved for the hardness of their hearts."

This anger, *orgé*, is essentially "settled opposition of God's holy nature against sin," and is often translated as "the wrath of God" (John 3:36 and elsewhere). God's children are commended to it, "Be ye angry and sin not" (Eph. 4:26). It is in contrast to *thumos*, the emotions of vehement fury, self-centered, explosive, and uncontrolled. We often call this a bad temper. Herod exhibited it: "When he saw that he was mocked of the wise men, was exceeding wroth, and sent forth, and slew all the children that were in Bethlehem, . . . from two years old and under" (Matt. 2:16). For this anger there is certainly no place in the Spirit-filled man.

4. Moods

Heaviness and darkness are treated by some as synonymous. But the Scripture does not. Darkness has no place with the victorious life. In 1 John 1:5-6 we read, "God is light, and in him is no darkness at all. If we say that we have fellowship with him, and walk in darkness, we lie, and do not the truth." It is sin that brings darkness. Hence sin is spoken of as "the unfruitful works of darkness" (Eph. 5:11), with which we are to have no fellowship. The child of God has been called "out of darkness into his marvelous light."

Sin, indeed, beclouds the vision of the soul and shuts out the light of God. To say that the soul is in darkness is equivalent to saying that sin has entered the heart and life and so broken the fellowship between the soul and God that the soul is left in darkness to grope his way. This is not the lot of the true child of God.

On the other hand, while "seasons of darkness" have no place in the heart of God's child it is well to distinguish between "darkness" and "heaviness." In 1 Peter 1:5-6 we read of a people "who are kept by the power of God through faith unto salvation ready to be revealed in the last time, whereby ye greatly rejoice, though now for a season, if need be, ye are in heaviness through manifold temptations." Sin brings darkness. Temptation brings heaviness ("distress," NASB, "grief," NIV). Unless one makes a difference between the two he is in danger of making spiritual shipwreck. For Satan will take advantage of our moods. He will whisper and cajole. Temptations will bring their heaviness and distress. But this should never be allowed to mar one's experience, or cause one to think he has lost divine favor. Never should it be allowed to bring darkness.

Man is a creature of moods. Everyone has temporary changes of a state of mind. It is when the moods get beyond bounds that they are distressing. But sorrow, joy, excitement, even ecstacy may come and go within the God-ordered life of a sanctified Christian. And it is the Spirit who will keep these moods within bounds.

5. Memory

Memory is not erased by the coming of the Holy Spirit. The mind stores all learning through the years. This fact in itself is a strong incentive to consistent Christian living from the days of youth. For while God assures us that "I will forgive their iniquity, and I will remember their sin no more" (Jer. 31:34), yet our own mind recalls them. I think of a godly man who declared to me recently: "Oh, that I could forget the days of my sinfulness. But I can't. They haunt me."

But memory can be overcast by godly deliberations. One of the most profound, practical exhortations given by Paul is the exhortation to positive thinking, found in Phil. 4:8, "Now brothers, practice thinking on what is true, what is honorable, what is right, what is pure, what is lovable, what is high-toned, yes, on everything that is excellent or praiseworthy" (Williams). And this we can do when the Spirit directs our thoughts, fills our moments of meditation, fires our desires.

6. Christian Perfection

Possibly one of the most provocative tension points is that of Christian perfection. Jesus commanded, for example, "Be ye therefore perfect, even as your Father which is in heaven is perfect" (Matt. 5:48). Now perfection is that state which cannot be improved. There is no comparative or superlative degree to "perfect" or "more perfect" or "most perfect." Then how can the Spirit-filled man, who indeed is yet human, be perfect? The answer must lie in the element in which he is to be perfect.

Man's perfection lies not in accomplishment, but in spirit; not in performance, but in purpose. It is to *Christian* perfection that God calls us, not to *sinless* perfection. Sinless perfection says that one is *not able to sin.* Christian perfection declares that he is *able not to sin.* And therein lies a world of difference. Sinless perfection would lift a person out of the world of reality, out of his normal human nature, out of a world of decision and responsibility. That, God would never do. But the ability both to sin and not to sin, puts upon the believer a challenging responsibility of choice, together with a divinely given provision.

It is to this that 1 John 2:1-2 speaks as John says, "My little children, these things write I unto you, that ye sin not. And if any man sin, we have an advocate with the Father, Jesus Christ the righteous: and he is the propitiation for our sins: and not for ours only, but also for the sins of the whole world." The tense of both of the verbs *sin* is aorist, the tense of point action. Jamieson, Fausset, and Brown puts it, "In order that ye may not sin at all," then quotes Alford, "The Greek aorist implying the absence not only of the habit, but of *single acts of sin*" (p. 527). The NEB recognizes the second usage, "But should anyone *commit a sin*." Thus: "My little children, these things I write unto you, that ye sin not at all. But if anyone commit a sin . . . " Indeed, the standard which God sets is high. No sin is excusable, or "to be expected."

But if an inadvertent sin is committed there is the immediate recourse of both an Advocate and a Propitiation—Jesus Christ the righteous. One need not go on to a second expression of the sin. And he can immediately find forgiveness and deliverance. That is the case of victorious living.

Although one's judgment and perception will improve under the tutelage of the Spirit, the treasure of the Holy Spirit's presence does not provide perfect judgment, or complete perception. If this were not true there would be no need of committees or councils in Christian administration. The presence of the Holy Spirit does not negate the repeated admonition of Proverbs, "Where no counsel is, the people fall; but in the multitude of counsellors there is safety," and "The way of a fool is right in his own eyes; but he that hearkeneth unto counsel is wise" (Prov. 11:14 and 12:15).

David's admonition to Solomon on the occasion of his taking over the throne is a pertinent charge to all: "Solomon, my son, know thou the God of thy father, and serve him with a *perfect heart* and a *willing mind*" (1 Chron. 28:9, italics added). And this is the more applicable when we remember that years before God had declared to Samuel, "The Lord seeth not as man seeth; for man looketh on the outward appearance, but the Lord looketh on the heart" (1 Sam. 16:7). There is a perfection of the heart with its intent and purpose, a willingness of the mind to be enlightened and instructed.

It is an awesome thing to serve God with a perfect heart—a perfect intent, purpose, dedication, surrender—when we know He looks not on the outward appearance, but on the heart. But it is also an encouraging situation. For God knows that the frailty of our judgment and our understanding, indeed, of our performance is due to the fact that "we have this treasure in earthen vessels." For "the Lord formed man of the dust of the ground, and breathed into his nostrils the breath of life; and man became a living soul" (Gen. 2:7). And therefore "he remembereth that we are dust" (Ps. 103:14).

It was in the light of all of this that Paul coined a meaningful word to express our limitations—*amemptōs*, variously translated as "unblameably" in KJV, "blameless" or "without blame" in NASB, NIV, and RSV. This in a holiness testimony, he confidently applied to his own manner of life: "Ye are witnesses, and God also, how holily and justly and unblameably we behaved ourselves among you that believe" (1 Thess. 2:10). But more particularly he wrote of the standard of holy living which one might achieve by God's gracious provision: "The very God of peace sanctify you wholly; and I pray God your whole spirit and soul and body be preserved blameless unto the coming of our Lord Jesus Christ" (1 Thess. 5:23).

Note that the word is "unblameably" not "faultlessly." A regrettable misinterpretation of the word is found in *The Living Bible* (Eph. 1:4). Faultless says flawless, without mistakes. This level we can never reach this side of glory (Jude 24), because of mistaken judgment, limited understanding, lack of comprehension. But blameless speaks of being innocent, guiltless, without condemnation. Those whose hearts are established "unblameable in holiness before God" (1 Thess. 3:13).

Thus Christian perfection is the perfection

Not Necessarily of	But Rather of
performance	purpose
accomplishments	intent
knowledge	dedication
understanding	surrender
angelic perfection	obedience
Adamic perfection	love
being faultless	being blameless
sinless perfection	Christian perfection
being unable to sin	being able not to sin

There is a mistaken concept gained by many regarding Paul's supposed denial of "perfection" as witnessed to in Phil. 3:13-14:

> Not as though I had already attained, either were already perfect: but I follow after, if that I may apprehend that for which also I am apprehended of Christ Jesus. Brethren, I count not myself to have apprehended: but this one thing I do, forgetting those things which are behind, and reaching forth unto those things which are before, I press toward the mark for the prize of the high calling of God in Christ Jesus.

The question regarding this perfection can quickly be settled, however, by referring back to the previous two verses, 10 and 11: "That I may know him, and the power of his resurrection, and the fellowship of his sufferings, being made conformable unto his death; if by any means I might attain unto the resurrection of the dead."

It is from this that he continues "Not as though I had already attained" such a resurrection "but I follow after," and eagerly "I press toward the mark for the prize of the high calling of God in Christ Jesus." Paul's "perfection" would be consummated in his resurrection. The same usage of the verb *teleioō* was made by Jesus when He said, "The third day I *shall be perfected*" (Luke 13:32, italics added), an obvious reference to a completion which was to come through His own resurrection. NASB and NIV translate it as "the third day I reach my goal." It is echoed by the same verb in our Lord's final cry, "It is finished."

As George A. Turner observes, "Paul does not mean perfect in an evangelical sense; rather he is not made perfect in the eschatological sense of the resurrection."[1]

It is related to Paul's expressed wish, again with the same verb: "That I *may finish* my course with joy, and the ministry, which I have received of the Lord Jesus" (Acts 20:24, italics added), and his anticipatory testimony "I have finished my course" (2 Tim. 4:7).

There is, additionally, in Phil. 3:15, a confusing use of the adjective "perfect," *teleios*: "Let us therefore, as many as be perfect, be thus minded." Here this is better translated by NIV and NASB margin as "mature," and in Heb. 5:14 "of full age" (KJV), "mature" (NASB, NIV).

7. Impossible Standards

Not unrelated to other tension points is that of apparently unreasonable standards expected from the spiritual man.

In a printed leaflet dated May, 1940, "Recognition of the Holy Spirit," written by my father, the late Colonel Fletcher Agnew, this subject is excellently dealt with. It is quoted herewith in full.

> Many Christians fail to seek the blessing of Holiness and the baptism with the Holy Spirit because they feel that it is an impossible standard of Christian life for them to attain or to maintain. They feel that they can maintain by constant effort and prayer a standard of justification or of salvation, but not of Holiness.
>
> They feel that Jesus, having been human, knows their temptations, limitations and frailties and is always ready to forgive their shortcomings. But to profess Holiness and to live a life pleasing to the Holy Spirit they consider to be outside of the realm of pos-

141

sibility. Their idea of the Holy Spirit is well illustrated by a chapter in my boyhood life.

At the time of my father's death, there were seven children in our family, the eldest only fourteen. My mother was a saint, saved, sanctified, full of the Holy Spirit, but she was, at the same time, sweetly human, and as indulgent as was consistent with the highest standards of Christian living. We children had much joy, stacks of fun on the farm, and were not hampered with unnecessary rules or red tape.

After my father's death, it was necessary for my mother to go away to a relative to recuperate from the strain of my father's last illness. Her sister, my Aunt Mary, was left in charge. Though she never had any children of her own, yet she thought she knew just how children should be trained. She considered we were all spoiled by an overindulgent mother and proceeded to make us model children according to her own standards during the month of our mother's absence. She had a hawk-eye, a keen nose, and a sharp tongue, and no small failings or faults were overlooked or condoned. Manners must be perfect, hands, necks and ears must be spotless, hats and clothes when taken off must always be hung in the proper place. We found we were under "law," and not under "grace." That month seemed a year before the return of our mother with her love and sweet harmony and peace.

Now, many Christians think the Holy Spirit is like Aunt Mary, a hard disciplinarian, exacting and difficult to please, easily grieved and often offended. But exactly the opposite is the truth.

While we would not lower the high standards of Holiness, yet, it is true as we read in Romans 8:21 when we are filled with the Spirit we are "delivered from bondage into the glorious liberty of the Children of God." While it is true that "they that are in the flesh (slaves of fleshly appetites and desires) cannot please God" (Romans 8:8), yet, it is also true that "as many as are led by the Spirit of God, they are the sons of God" (Romans 8:14). And "where the Spirit of the Lord is, there is liberty" (2 Corinthians 3:17).

The relationship of the Holy Spirit to the one in

whom He dwells is not that of schoolmaster to pupil, or of an exacting aunt to an irrepressible, adolescent nephew, but of a loving, wise, understanding mother, unselfishly solicitous for the supreme happiness, highest development and greatest usefulness of her own child.

To refuse the most complete and perfect communion of the Holy Spirit with our Spirit is but to refuse entrance into the innermost circle of our being by One Who alone can make us supremely happy, useful, successful and Christ-like.

11/

WALKING BY THE SPIRIT

"If we live by the Spirit, let us also walk by the Spirit
. . . And those who will walk by this rule, peace and mercy
be upon them, and upon the Israel of God" (Gal. 5:25; 6:16,
NASB). Within this paragraph, encompassed by this exhortation and this promise, are enclosed eternal truths
related to "walking by the Spirit."

Both life and holiness are the work of the one Holy
Spirit. He who operates in establishing the new birth
(John 3:6-8) also operates in the sanctification of holy living (1 Pet. 1:2). Since we are made alive by the Spirit, "if
[since] we live by the Spirit," we are exhorted also to practice a life of ordered holiness by the Spirit's power and
through His very presence—"Let us also walk by the
Spirit."

Many know that they have received spiritual life

through faith, but think they can secure sanctification by works and religious formalities. This is a great error. It never brings victory. Believing in Christ for sanctification as well as for regeneration through the work of the Holy Spirit introduces one into a life of power and victory.

It surely was something of this which inspired Edward Harland to write the song:

O for a humbler walk with God!
  Lord, bend this stubborn heart of mine;
Subdue each rising, rebel thought,
  And all my will conform to Thine.

O for a holier walk with God!
  A heart from all pollution free;
Expel, O Lord, each sinful love,
  And fill my soul with love to Thee.

O for a nearer walk with God!
  Lord, turn my wandering heart to Thee;
Help me to live by faith in Him
  Who lived and died and rose for me.

Lord, send Thy Spirit from above
  With light and love and power divine;
And by His all-constraining grace
  Make me and keep me ever Thine.

1. Walking by the Spirit

The very verb Paul uses here is instructive. *Stoicheō* (from *stoikos*, a row), is literally "to walk by a rule," "to walk in line," especially, Vine says, this is a marching to battle, in line, in step, in fellowship with the Spirit. It is, he says, "an exhortation to keep step with another in submission of heart to the Holy Spirit, the great means of unity and harmony in a church." It is used instead of the more common *peripateō*, "to walk" (5:16), which stresses

145

outward conduct. Thus, to "walk *(stoicheō)* by the Spirit" is *to live one's whole life in accordance with the mind of Christ. Christ.* The verb has some element of a military formation, yet speaks of common interests, of comradeship, of close communion. This is the force of the word Paul chooses to use here.

The account of the Early Church as recorded in the Book of Acts is truly the account of those who walked by this rule, who walked in line, in step, in fellowship with the Spirit.

Scarcely a chapter of the Book of Acts goes by without giving a thrilling account of those who "walked by the Spirit." With Him they were filled (2:4; 4:8, 31; 6:3, 5; 7:55; 9:17; 11:24; 13:9, 52); baptized (Acts 1:4; 11:16); and empowered (4:31, 33). Fearful disciples (John 20:19) became charged with courage and boldness (Acts 4:13, 29, 31; 9:29; 14:3; 18:26; 19:8). They were no longer alone, but were enjoying "the communion of the Holy Spirit." By Him they were "ordained" (Acts 20:28), "comforted" (9:31), and made "fervent" (18:25). They were "in step" with the Holy Spirit.

A willing Philip, having been directed by an angel to race toward the Ethopian's chariot, was commanded by the Spirit to climb in, and to expound the meaning of the 53rd chapter of Isaiah. He thus led the man to Christ, only to be snatched away by the Spirit to Azotus for still further ministry. The Holy Spirit directed Peter to the home of Cornelius in Antioch, much against his will, but the result was the resounding conversion of an entire household. The Holy Spirit singled out Barnabas and Saul, and sent them on their important mission of missionary evangelism. He restrained Paul and Timothy from going to Asia, but sent them instead to Europe, a choice, as it turned out, of astonishing significance to the whole world. He supervised the decision of the first church council in

Jerusalem so that from it went out the message to the Gentiles everywhere. "It seemed good to the Holy Spirit and to us." The Early Church indeed learned to walk, to "march to battle in line" with the Holy Spirit. The pattern was set for all time.

2. Walking with the Saints

But this "walking by the Spirit," this "fellowship of the Spirit" was not just between the believers and the Spirit. In a very practical way it was among themselves as well. Spirit-filled men found themselves walking not only "in step" with, or "in line with," the Holy Spirit, but also in step with their fellow believers. There is no richer account in print relative to Christian fellowship and true communion than that found in the early chapters of Acts regarding the Jerusalem church.

> Those who had received his word were baptized; and there were added that day about three thousand souls. And they were continually devoting themselves to the apostles' teaching and to fellowship, to the breaking of bread and to prayer.
>
> And everyone kept feeling a sense of awe; and many wonders and signs were taking place through the apostles. And all those who had believed were together, and had all things in common; and they began selling their property and possessions, and were sharing them with all, as anyone might have need. And day by day continuing with one mind in the temple, and breaking bread from house to house, they were taking their meals together with gladness and sincerity of heart, praising God, and having favor with all the people. And the Lord was adding to their number day by day those who were being saved (Acts 2:41-47, NASB).

And again:

> When they had prayed, the place where they had gathered together was shaken, and they were all filled

with the Holy Spirit, and began to speak the word of God with boldness.

And the congregation of those who believed were of one heart and soul; and not one of them claimed that anything belonging to him was his own; but all things were common property to them. And with great power the apostles were giving witness to the resurrection of the Lord Jesus, and abundant grace was upon them all. For there was not a needy person among them, for all who were owners of lands or houses would sell them and bring the proceeds of the sales, and lay them at the apostles' feet; and they would be distributed to each, as any had need (Acts 4:31-35, NASB).

3. Walking "with one accord"

It was in a climate like this that there was coined the meaningful, effective phrase "with one accord." Essentially this expression is unique to the Book of Acts and reveals a product of the indwelling Holy Spirit. It is the translation of the single Greek word *homothumadon,* expressing the unity of minds and purpose in a strong, almost passionate union. The word is from *homos,* "the same," and *thumos,* "mind, passion." The disciples first came together in that vigorous bond "of one accord" when seeking in prayer and supplication "the promise of the Father" (Acts 1:14). They were found in the same tie of fellowship daily "with one accord" in the temple and as they went out "from house to house" taking their meals together (2:46). In the shadow of the first severe opposition they came together, lifing up their voices to God in fervent appeal "with one accord" (4:24). In the searing light of a Spirit-filled evangelistic crusade by Philip, the people of Samaria gave heed "with one accord" to the message and miracles he presented (8:6). After "much disputing" at the first church conference those assembled finally came "to one accord" with their message to the Gentiles (15:25).

4. Walking According to Holy Exhortation

Paul was admonishing all "spiritual" Christians in his letter to the Galatian church, particularly in the verses 5:25—6:16. Here he uses the word *stoicheō*, "*Let us walk* by the Spirit" (5:25) and "Those who *will walk* by this rule" (6:16, italics added both times). Let us examine that segment of the Epistle.

The present imperative of the opening exhortation carries the sense of continued, habitual conduct. "If [or "since," NIV] we live by the Spirit, let us also [habitually] walk by the Spirit." To this exhortation Paul puts first a note of warning, and then a challenge, surely not confined to the people of Galatia.

> Let us not become boastful, challenging one another, envying one another. Brethren, even if a man is caught in any trespass, you who are spiritual, restore such a one in a spirit of gentleness, looking to yourself, lest you too be tempted. Bear one another's burdens, and thus fulfil the law of Christ (5:26—6:2, NASB).

This disciplined life of the spiritual believer will show the fruit of the Spirit—gentleness—toward a fellow believer, even though he has been surprised—"caught"— in a "trespass." The King James translation identifies this "trespass" *(paraptoma)* as "a fault," and Robertson in *Word Pictures,* observes that it is "a slip, or lapse rather than a willful sin."[1] It could be a relapse into boasting, envy, or a comparable fault. Restoration, healing, mending will be applied by the "spiritual" ones, the Spirit-filled Christians, with the humble realization that such a lapse might come to any one of them as well. It is a good practice to "bear with one another" in their lapses, their faults, their trespasses, "and thus fulfill the law of Christ." This law has just been delineated in 5:14: "The whole Law is fulfilled in one word, in the statement, 'You shall love your neighbor as yourself' " (NASB).

Further, this walk by the Spirit allows for no conceit, but demands individual responsibility. Paul continues his criterion: "If anyone thinks he is something when he is nothing, he deceives himself. But let each one examine his own work, and then he will have reason for boasting in regard to himself alone, and not in regard to another. For each one shall bear his own load" (Gal. 6:3-5, NASB).

This walk by the Spirit also requires, in a practical vein, an unselfish sharing of God's good things with teachers, and with all men. It exacts just penalties for irresponsible planting, but rich rewards for sowing to the Spirit.

> Let the one who is taught the word share all good things with him who teaches. Do not be deceived, God is not mocked; for whatever a man sows, this he will also reap. For the one who sows to his own flesh shall from the flesh reap corruption, but the one who sows to the Spirit shall from the Spirit reap eternal life. And let us not lose heart in doing good, for in due time we shall reap if we do not grow weary. So then, while we have opportunity, let us do good to all men, and especially to those who are of the household of the faith (Gal. 6:6-10, NASB).

This "march to battle in line" with the Holy Spirit is, above all, a *spiritual* pattern of life. Outward, physical ceremonies, a "showing in the flesh," a dependence upon religious rituals, even sacraments, are not compatible with it. Indeed, this walking by the Spirit calls for an actual fellowship *on* the cross with Christ, a crucifixion of self. And this Paul would emphasize by writing this out in his own large printing. Note the following:

> See with what large letters I am writing to you with my own hand. Those who desire to make a good showing in the flesh try to compel you to be circumcised, simply that they may not be persecuted for the cross of Christ. For those who are circumcised do not even keep the Law themselves, but they desire to have

you circumcised, that they may boast in your flesh. But may it never be that I should boast, except in the cross of our Lord Jesus Christ, through which the world has been crucified to me, and I to the world. For neither is circumcision anything, nor uncircumcision, but a new creation (Gal. 6:11-15, NASB).

To this Paul adds his final blessing and benediction: "Those who will walk by this rule, peace and mercy be upon them, and upon the Israel of God. From now on let no one cause trouble for me, for I bear on my body the brand-marks of Jesus" (Gal. 6:16-17, NASB).

Indeed, if we live by the Spirit, let us also walk by the Spirit, in the orderly array of a disciplined life!

Commissioner Brengle wrote from Boston on October 1, 1913:

Our glory and strength are found, not in splendid temples and vast cathedrals, but in union with Christ, in sharing His cross, in bearing His burdens, in possessing His lowly, loving, sacrificial Spirit. If we have this Spirit we shall go from strength to strength; we shall pass on a heritage of faith and love and holy example to our children. We shall have a crown of life, a crown of life that fadeth not away. We shall see Jesus. We shall be like Him—and we shall be satisfied. Hallelujah!

William Cowper gives us words for our prayer in his song:

O for a closer walk with God,
    A calm and heavenly frame,
A light to shine upon the road
    That leads me to the Lamb!

Return, O holy Dove, return
    Sweet Messenger of rest!
I hate the sins that made Thee mourn,
    And drove Thee from my breast.

So shall my walk be close with God,
Calm and serene my frame;
So purer light shall mark the road
That leads me. to the Lamb.

Reference Notes

Chapter 2:

1. G. Abbott-Smith, *A Manual Greek Lexicon of the New Testament* (Edinburgh: T. & T. Clark, 1950), p. 144.

Chapter 3:

1. Robert Jamieson, A. R. Fausset, and David Brown, *Commentary on the Whole Bible* (Grand Rapids: Zondervan Publishing House, n.d.), p. 13.

2. Charles W. Carter, ed., *Wesleyan Bible Commentary* (Grand Rapids: William B. Eerdmans Publishing Co., 1964), 5:395.

Chapter 4:

1. *The Salvation Army Handbook of Doctrine* (St. Albans, England: Campfield Press, 1969), p. 154.

2. H. Orton Wiley, *Christian Theology* (Kansas City: Beacon Hill Press, 1958), 2:317.

3. W. E. Vine, *Expository Dictionary of New Testament Words* (Westwood, N.J.: Fleming H. Revell Co., 1958), p. 147.

4. *Ibid.*, p. 108.

Chapter 5:

1. Charles W. Carter, *The Person and Ministry of the Holy Spirit* (Grand Rapids: Baker Book House, 1974), p. 207.

2. Wayne A. Robinson, *I Once Spoke in Tongues* (Westwood, N.J.: Fleming H. Revell Co., 1975), p. 173.

3. John Sherrill, *They Speak with Other Tongues* (New York: McGraw-Hill, 1964), p. 33.

Chapter 6:

1. Vine, *Expository Dictionary of New Testament Words*, p. 214.

2. H. E. Dana and Julius R. Mantey, *A Manual Grammar of the Greek New Testament* (New York: The Macmillan Co., 1947), p. 156.

3. Wesley L. Duewel, *The Holy Spirit and Tongues* (Winona Lake, Ind.: Light and Life Press, 1974), p. 52.

4. *Interpreter's Bible* (Nashville: Abingdon Press, 1951), 12:71.

5. Frank Bartleman, *How Pentecost Came to Los Angeles* (Privately printed, 1925), p. 88.

6. W. T. Purkiser, R. S. Taylor, and Willard H. Taylor, *God, Man, and Salvation* (Kansas City: Beacon Hill Press of Kansas City, 1977), p. 43.

Chapter 7:

1. George A. Turner and Julius R. Mantey, *The Gospel of John* (Grand Rapids: William B. Eerdmans Publishing Co., 1964), pp. 184-85.

2. Carter, *The Wesleyan Bible Commentary,* 5:202. See also his *The Person and Ministry of the Holy Spirit,* p. 285.

3. Ralph Earle, *Evangelical Commentary on Mark* (Grand Rapids: Zondervan Publishing House, 1957), p. 30.

Chapter 9:

1. Earle, *Evangelical Commentary on Mark,* p. 30.

2. Samuel L. Brengle, *When the Holy Ghost Is Come* (New York: The Salvation Army, 1918), p. 23.

3. C. W. Ruth, *Entire Sanctification, a Second Blessing* (Chicago and Boston: The Christian Witness Co., 1903), p. 52.

4. Wiley, *Christian Theology,* 2:321.

5. *The Salvation Army Handbook of Doctrine,* p. 151.

Chapter 10:

1. Carter, ed., *Wesleyan Bible Commentary,* 5:473.

Chapter 11:

1. A. T. Robertson, *Word Pictures in the New Testament* (New York: Richard R. Smith, Inc., 1930), 4:315.

Bibliography

Abbott-Smith, G. *A Manual Greek Lexicon of the New Testament.* Edinburgh: T. & T. Clark, 1950.

Brengle, Samuel Logan. *When the Holy Ghost Is Come.* New York: The Salvation Army, 1918.

Carter, Charles W., ed. *The Wesleyan Bible Commentary.* Grand Rapids: William B. Eerdmans Publishing Co., 1964.

————. *The Person and Ministry of the Holy Spirit.* Grand Rapids: Baker Book House, 1974.

Dana, H. E., and Mantey, Julius R. *A Manual Grammar of the Greek New Testament.* New York: The Macmillan Co., 1947.

Duewel, Wesley L. *The Holy Spirit and Tongues.* Winona Lake, Ind.: Light and Life Press, 1974.

Earle, Ralph. *Evangelical Commentary on Mark.* Grand Rapids: Zondervan Publishing House, 1957.

Funk and Wagnalls. *Standard College Dictionary.* New York: Harper and Row, Publishers, 1977.

Gromacki, Robert G. *The Modern Tongues Movement.* Philadelphia: Presbyterian and Reformed Publishing Co., 1967.

Gustafson, Robert R. *Author of Confusion.* Tampa, Fla.: Grace Publishing Co., 1971.

The Interpreter's Bible. New York: Abingdon-Cokesbury Press, 1951.

Jamieson, Robert; Fausset, A. R.; and Brown, David. *A Commentary on the Whole Bible.* Grand Rapids: Zondervan Publishing House, n.d.

Jorstad, Erling. *The Holy Spirit in Today's Church.* Nashville: Abingdon Press, 1973.

Kelsey, Morton. *Encounter with God.* Minneapolis, Minn.: Bethany Fellowship, Inc., 1972.

Mills, Watson E. *Speaking in Tongues: Let's Talk About It.* Waco, Tex.: Word Books, 1973.

Oke, Norman R. *Facing the Tongues Issue.* Kansas City: Beacon Hill Press of Kansas City, 1973.

Pulkingham, Graham. *Gathered for Power.* New York: Morehouse-Barlow Co., 1972.

Purkiser, W. T. *The Gifts of the Spirit.* Kansas City: Beacon Hill Press of Kansas City, 1975.

Purkiser, W. T.; Taylor, Richard S.; and Taylor, Willard H. *God, Man, and Salvation.* Kansas City: Beacon Hill Press of Kansas City, 1977.

Robertson, Archibald Thomas. *Word Pictures in the New Testament.* New York: Richard R. Smith, Inc., 1930.

Robinson, Wayne A. *I Once Spoke in Tongues.* Westwood, N.J.: Fleming H. Revell Co., 1975.

Ruth, C. W. *Entire Sanctification, a Second Blessing.* Chicago: The Christian Witness Co., 1903.

The Salvation Army Song Book. New York: The Salvation Army Supplies Department, 1954.

Sherrill, John. *They Speak with Other Tongues.* New York: McGraw-Hill Co., 1964.

Taylor, Richard S. *Tongues: Their Purpose and Meaning.* Kansas City: Beacon Hill Press of Kansas City, 1973.

Turner, George A., and Mantey, Julius R. *The Gospel of John.* Grand Rapids: William B. Eerdmans Publishing Co., 1964.

Vine, W. E. *Expository Dictionary of New Testament Words.* Westwood, N.J.: Fleming H. Revell Co., 1958.

Wiley, H. Orton. *Christian Theology,* 3 vols. Kansas City: Beacon Hill Press, 1958 edition.

Scripture Index

158

159

160